P9-EDV-305

In group

class struggle

Sociology

2.²⁰

THE FUNCTIONS
OF SOCIAL CONFLICT

LEWIS A. COSER

The Functions
of Social Conflict

THE FREE PRESS OF GLENCOE

COLLIER-MACMILLAN LIMITED, *London*

CAMROSE LUTHERAN COLLEGE
LIBRARY

Copyright © 1956 by The Free Press, a Corporation

Printed in the United States of America

All rights reserved. No part of this book may be reproduced or utilized in any form or by any means, electronic or mechanical, including photocopying, recording or by any information, storage and retrieval system, without permission in writing from the Publisher.

FIRST FREE PRESS PAPERBACK EDITION 1964

For information, address:
The Free Press of Glencoe
A Division of The Macmillan Company
The Crowell-Collier Publishing Company
60 Fifth Avenue, New York, N.Y., 10011

Collier-Macmillan Canada, Ltd., Toronto, Ontario

DESIGNED BY SIDNEY SOLOMON

Library of Congress Catalog Card Number: 56-6874

FOR ROSE

PREFACE

THIS BOOK IS AN EFFORT to clarify the concept of *social conflict*, and in so doing to examine the use of this concept in empirical sociological research.

Concepts may be thought of as being neither true nor false; they are apt or inept, clear or vague, fruitful or useless. They are tools designed to capture relevant aspects of reality and thus "constitute the definitions (or prescriptions) of what is to be observed."[1]

Before the "facts" can speak, they have to be arranged through some conceptual scheme. The divorce between research, conceived as a quest for "facts," and theories which too often soar beyond the reach of facts, is responsible for many of the shortcomings of American sociology. And this divorce is responsible as well for the lack of cumulation and continuity in American sociology. Periodic conceptual analysis, in our view, serves to mitigate these two kinds of shortcomings.

This study seeks to clarify and to consolidate conceptual schemes which are pertinent to data of social conflict. It does not present the results of new research, but it hopes to stimulate such research. By taking stock of past contributions, it aims to advance the formulation of future inquiries.

Although the concept of social conflict is of central importance for an understanding of major areas of social relations, it has been almost wholly neglected by American sociologists in recent years. The writer has attempted elsewhere[2] to seek the reasons for this neglect in the changes, over the last fifty years or so, of the socially molded images which American sociologists have had of themselves and in changes of their actual or potential audience. The first chapter of this book will summarize some of these findings. The interested reader is referred to the more comprehensive study.

This book deals mainly with a number of basic propositions which have been distilled from theories of social conflict, in particular from the theories of Georg Simmel. These propositions are in turn extended by being related to other findings of a theoretical or empirical nature.

Social conflict has been defined in various ways. For the purpose of this study, it will provisionally be taken to mean a struggle over values and claims to scarce status, power and resources in which the aims of the opponents are to neutralize, injure or eliminate their rivals. This working definition serves only as a point of departure.

Our concern is mainly with the functions, rather than the dysfunctions, of social conflict, that is to say, with those consequences of social conflict which make for an increase rather than a decrease in the adaptation or adjustment of particular social relationships or groups. Far from being only a "negative" factor which "tears apart," social conflict may fulfill a number of determinate functions in groups and other interpersonal relations; it may, for example, contribute to the maintenance of group boundaries and prevent the withdrawal of members from a group. Commitment to the view that social conflict is necessarily destructive of the relationship within which it occurs leads, as we shall see, to highly deficient interpretations. To focus on the functional aspects of social conflict is not to deny that certain forms of conflict are indeed destructive of group unity or that they lead to disintegration of specific social structures. Such focusing serves, however, to correct a balance of analysis which has been tilted in the other direction.[3]

"I say that those who cavil at the dissension betwixt the Patricians and Plebeians, cavil at the very causes which in my opinion contributed most to [Rome's] liberty; for whilst they object to them as the sources of tumult and confusion, they do not consider the good effects they produced; seeming either to forget, or never to have known, that in all Commonwealths, the views and dispositions of the Nobility and Commonalty must of necessity be very widely if not totally different; and that all the laws which are made in favour of liberty, have been owing to the difference betwixt them."

Niccolo Machiavelli, *Political Discourses*,
Book I, Chapter IV

"The clash of doctrines is not a disaster, it is an opportunity."

Alfred North Whitehead, *Science and the Modern World*

"It is the bad side that produces the movement that makes history, by providing a struggle."

Karl Marx, *The Poverty of Philosophy*

ACKNOWLEDGMENTS

THIS STUDY could not have been written without the teaching, astute criticism, and friendly advice and consultation of Professor Robert K. Merton. My gratitude to him is of a kind which can hardly be expressed adequately in the form of a simple acknowledgment.

With my wife, Rose L. Coser of Wellesley College, I have for many years shared a working partnership based on a common faith and made perfect by marriage. By rights this volume should have been published under our joint authorship, since large portions of it owe so much to her analytical skills. Her constant encouragement and challenging criticism were invaluable.

My friends, Gertrude McPherson, formerly of Wellesley College, and James McPherson, formerly of Smith College, were of considerable help in the editing of an earlier version of this study. I am deeply grateful to them.

Professors Richard Hofstadter, Seymour M. Lipset, Robert S. Lynd, and David B. Truman of Columbia University read an earlier version of this book and made a number of most valuable critical comments. Several of my colleagues at Brandeis University, especially Professors Frank Manuel and Bernard Rosenberg (now of Harpur College), read the manuscript and gave helpful criticism.

Special thanks are due to Amber Harrington who has been most helpful in compiling the index and reading proof.

Finally, it is a pleasure to record my indebtedness to my friends, Jeremiah Kaplan and Ned Polsky of the Free Press. Without their interest and co-operation this study might not have been published.

LEWIS A. COSER

Waltham, Mass.,
February 1956

CONTENTS

[*13*]

CONTENTS

CHAPTER I

INTRODUCTORY

ONE OF THE FIRST MEETINGS (1907) of the newly organized American Sociological Society had *Social Conflict* as its main topic of discussion. The central paper was read by the Social Darwinist Thomas N. Carver. Said Carver: "There may be many cases where there is a complete harmony of interests, but these give rise to no problems and therefore we do not need to concern ourselves about them."[1] Carver felt that only where disharmony and antagonism prevailed could one speak at all of a moral and of a scientific problem.

It is significant that in the discussion which followed, in which most leading sociologists of the time—Giddings, Ross, Ward, Hayes, among others—participated, almost no one questioned the importance that Carver had assigned to the study of conflict. The only objections concerned his rigid economic interpretation.

At the twenty-sixth annual meeting of the American Sociological Society in 1930, *Social Conflict* was again the main topic of discussion. By then, Howard W. Odum stated in his presidential address,[2] quoting another sociologist: "Social conflict is sociologically an unexplored field. . . . The sociology of conflict has yet to be written." But the session itself did little to fill the gap, and the proceedings gave the distinct impression that the study of social conflict was no longer considered a central concern by the members of the Society.

A generation later, Jessie Bernard, writing in the *American Journal of Sociology*,[3] asked once again: "Where is the modern sociology of conflict?" and went on to say that "since the time of such early pioneers as Small, Park, and Ross, little progress has been made. American sociologists in recent years have been content to leave the scientific study of conflict where Simmel left it."

Even a cursory examination of the contemporary work of American sociologists clearly indicates that conflict has been very much neglected indeed as a field of investigation. It is our contention, though we will here not be able to prove it fully, that this neglect of conflict is at least in part the result of changes that have occurred in the audience, roles and self-images of American sociologists. These shifts may be said to have contributed to a changing focus of attention—from concern with conflict to concern with such areas of sociological investigation as "consensus," "common value orientation" and the like.

I

It appears that the first generation of American sociologists saw themselves as reformers and addressed themselves to an audience of reformers. Such self-images and publics called attention to situations of conflict, and this accounts for the sociologists' concern with them. Furthermore, far from being viewed merely as a negative phenomenon, social conflict was seen as performing decidedly positive functions. In particular, conflict provided to these sociologists the central explanatory category for the analysis of social change and of "progress."

The reformist ethic so canalized the interest of the first generation of American sociologists as to constitute an important element in the enhanced cultivation of sociology. The deep-rooted reformist interests of the day demanded in their forceful implications the systematic, rational and empirical study of society and the control of a corrupt world.[4]

The predominance of the "problems," and hence melioristic, approach over the purely theoretical concern with sociology is clearly evident in the charter statements of the earlier departments of sociology. Even though American sociologists around the turn of the century attempted to achieve academic respectability by emphasizing the scientific and theoretical aspects of their work, the reformers' zeal was still not spent. To a modern sociologist, noting the almost complete separation, if not opposition, between social science and reform today, the recurrence of reformist phrases in the writings of the fathers of American sociology is apt to signify merely customary usage. But such an interpretation is possible only if one neglects to translate oneself within the framework of late nineteenth and early twentieth century values.[5] As Albion Small and George E. Vincent stated in the first textbook of American sociology: "Sociology was born of the modern ardor to improve society."[6]

Not all sociologists agreed as to the nature of needed reform. Of the leading figures of the time, Ward, Small, Ross, Veblen and Cooley may be said to have been "structural reformers," in that they advocated social changes so deep-going as to justify the statement that they would, if adopted, result in a change in the total structure of society and lead to the emergence of a new social system with different structural requirements. Sumner and Giddings, on the other hand, may be said to have been "detail reformers" in that they proposed measures which would make for adjustments within the institutional order but would not entail basic changes and would not involve the most relevant structural requirements of the system.

If we now turn from the self-image of the sociologist as a reformer to the audience of early sociologists, we note that it was predominantly a "reform audience." The term "reform audience" is here used in a rather broad sense. It is intended to cover all the movements and personalities that criticized some central aspects of the *status quo* and proposed remedies. Although there are vast differences between the Social Gospel movement and organized Marxist Socialism, although the devotees of Hull House and those of Eugene Debs frequently clashed, it seems justifiable to group all these movements together for the present purpose; they constituted a fairly homogeneous public insofar as they were held together by dissatisfaction with the *status quo*.

Those sociologists whom we have called "structural reformers" were also those who found their major non-academic audience above all among the radical Left of the day. This Left constituted the audience of Ward, Veblen, Ross, Small, and, probably, Cooley.

The audience of Giddings and Sumner, on the other hand, that is of sociologists concerned with partial reform only, consisted of powerful and right-thinking men, who, though deeply attached to the *status quo*, were conscious of the need for specific reforms in, say, municipal administration or tariff policy.

Turning now to the writings of early American sociologists, we notice that conflict is indeed a central category of their systems and that it is furthermore seen as a fundamental and constructive part of social organization. A view of society, and especially of social change, that did not include concern with conflict phenomena appeared to them seriously deficient. Whether it is Cooley stating "The more one thinks of it, the more he will see that conflict and co-operation are not separable things, but phases of one process which always involves something of both"[7] or "You can resolve the social order into a great number of co-operative wholes of various sorts, each of which includes conflicting elements within itself, upon which it is imposing some sort of harmony with a view to conflict with other wholes";[8] whether it is Small writing that ". . . in form, the social process is incessant reaction of persons prompted by interests that in part conflict with the interests of their fellows, and in part comport with the interests of others";[9] or Ross affirming that "In a way, open opposition preserves society . . . in any voluntary association the corking up of the protest and opposition of the rest . . . by the dominant element is likely to lead to the splitting of the group. . . . Opposition between groups hardens and toughens those which can stand the strain";[10] or Sumner laying down that "The relation of comradeship and peace in the we-group and that of hostility and war towards others-groups are correlative to each other";[11]—for all of them conflict was a central category.

When they felt that certain types of social conflict contained negative features, destructive of the social matrix, they stressed the need for structural reforms rather than "adjustment" to existing structural requirements.

The first generation of American sociologists addressed themselves to a public which was engaged in, advocated, and highly valued different types of conflict activities. This reference group gave to the representative sociological thinkers of the time positive response and recognition, thus reinforcing and sustaining their self-image. And since this public placed high positive valuation on conflict activities, the sociologists of that generation not only focused their attention upon conflict phenomena, but also tended to evaluate them positively. Conflict was seen as inherent in the social structure, and those particular types of conflict which were evaluated negatively could be eliminated, they felt, only through structural change. Thus even a negative evaluation of certain types of conflict pointed to the need for structural reform.

The generation of sociologists which was to follow that of the founders, especially the Chicago School, faced a somewhat different situation. The background and orientation of Robert E. Park, for example, does not seem to be essentially different from that of the earlier generation, but during the years after World War I, the audience already had changed to a considerable extent. As university research oriented itself to the demands of outside agencies, the public of the sociologist tended to shift. Park's writings, to give just one example, insofar as they penetrated beyond the academic community, were of vital interest to city reform and improvement associations as well as to race relations agencies, but seemed to have exerted little influence on the radical and reform public. Yet Park's theoretical work still falls into the pattern of the earlier contributions. Not only did he utilize "conflict" as one of his central and fundamental concepts, but he also stressed repeatedly its positive functions. In the *Introduction to the Science of Society*[12] by Park and Burgess, which outlined the programmatic orientation of the Chicago Department of Sociology, no less than seventy pages are devoted to a discussion of conflict. Conflict is ranked among the few basic forms of human interaction. Furthermore, Park felt: "Only where there is a conflict is behavior conscious and self-conscious; only here are the conditions for rational conduct."[13] To Park, conflict was not only the mechanism through which self-consciousness was achieved, it was in fact constitutive of any organized society: "Conflict," writes Park, "tends to bring about an integration and a superordination and subordination of the conflict groups."[14]

II

In contrast to the figures discussed so far, the majority of sociologists who dominate contemporary sociology, far from seeing themselves as reformers and addressing themselves to an audience of reformers, either have oriented themselves toward purely academic and professional audiences, or have attempted to find a hearing among decision-makers in public or private bureaucracies.

They center attention predominantly upon problems of adjustment rather than upon conflict; upon social statics rather than upon dynamics. Of key problematic importance to them has been the maintenance of existing structures and the ways and means of insuring their smooth functioning. They have focused upon maladjustments and tensions which interfere with consensus. Where the older generation discussed the need for structural change, the new generation deals with adjustment of individuals to given structures. In the dominant trend of contemporary American sociology, the psychological subsumes the structural and hence individual malfunctioning subsumes social conflict.[15]

While the earlier generation would in the main agree with Charles H. Cooley that "Conflict, of some sort, is the life of society, and progress emerges from a struggle in which individual, class, or institution seeks to realize its own idea of good,"[16] the contemporary generation has tended to replace analysis of conflict by the study of "tensions," "strains," and psychological malfunctioning.

The following discussion will deal with the work of Talcott

Parsons and to a lesser extent with other contemporary sociologists. In his detailed study the author has dealt more exhaustively with these other representative figures; the interested reader is referred to this study.[17]

A persistent theme runs through almost all of the writings of Talcott Parsons: concern with those elements in social structures that assure their maintenance. Although interest in the processes of social change is occasionally present in Parsons, such concern is distinctly marginal. It may be said that all of Parsons' work, beginning with *The Structure of Social Action*,[18] is an extended commentary on the Hobbesian question: How is social order possible?

While to an earlier generation of American sociologists, "laws" of social change, structural variability, and analysis of what later theorists called "functional alternatives"[19] were of central concern, these questions, although not totally neglected in Parsons' work, are peripheral to him. Although he is one of the foremost Weberian scholars in this country and has been deeply influenced by Weber's thought, his work in this respect seems more directly related to the Durkheimian quest for social cohesion in the face of threatening anomie than to the Weberian insistence that "conflict cannot be excluded from social life. . . . 'Peace' is nothing more than a change in the form of conflict or in the antagonists or in the objects of the conflict, or finally in the chances of selection."[20]

Parsons' sociological work grew out of his interest in the non-rational elements in economic behavior. What appeared problematic to Parsons were not the rational conflicts of interest that preoccupied classical political economists, but rather the non-rational, noncontractual elements in contract which had escaped their notice. Focusing on normative structures, which maintain and guarantee social order, Parsons was led to view conflict as having primarily disruptive, dissociating and dysfunctional consequences. Parsons considers conflict primarily a "disease." He feels with Shakespeare that "when degree is shaked . . . the enterprise is sicked."[21]

In an article on "Racial and Religious Differences as Factors in Group Tension,"[22] Parsons provides us with some clues to his thinking. After noting that modern men have begun to attack problems of social organization that seemed insoluble in earlier generations, the author compares such problems to physical illness. Just as we have made great strides, he asserts, in the control of sickness, so we can deal therapeutically with important factors in group antagonism although an "ultimate residue of tragic conflict of value and human helplessness" will remain. Since his paper deals mainly with racial and religious antagonisms, his emphasis on the disruptive elements in conflict might seem in part to derive from the particular conflict situations he is discussing; yet the analogy of sickness and conflict recurs in his other works.

Terminology often provides a clue to orientation. Parsons prefers to speak of "tensions" and "strains" where earlier theorists would have used the term "conflict," and this choice does not appear to be fortuitous. Both "tension" and "strain" connote injury due to overexertion, overtasking or excessive pressure, thus connoting some form of "sickness" in the system. With this in mind, we may examine the indexes of two recent volumes by Parsons. The *Essays*[23] contain sixteen entries under "strain" and twenty entries under "tension"; however, there are only nine entries under "social conflict," although there are additional entries under value conflict and emotional conflict. In the more recent *The Social System*[24] the entry "social conflict" has entirely disappeared, but there are seventeen entries under "strain."

In his only paper dealing specifically with class conflict[25] Parsons again uses medical analogy: "I believe," he says, "that class conflict is endemic in our modern industrial type of society. . . ." To Parsons class conflict is "endemic," like a disease. The medical analogy is still pushed further in an essay, "Propaganda and Social Control,"[26] where he attempts to establish a parallel between a medical man treating a sick patient and a propaganda specialist treating a sick society. Although conflict is not specifically discussed in this essay, it seems clear from the context that the author equates conflicting with deviant behavior, which is seen as a disease in need of treatment.

Parsons' general orientation has led him to view conflict as dysfunctional and disruptive and to disregard its positive functions. Conflict appears to him as a partly avoidable, partly inevitable and "endemic" form of sickness in the body social. It seems that Parsons' interest in mental health in recent years is to some extent explained by his concern with mechanisms of social control that minimize conflict, and by his conviction that psychoanalysts and other mental health specialists can play a significant role in reducing deviance.

While, by and large, the men of the earlier generation were concerned with progressive change in the social order, Parsons is primarily interested in the conservation of existing structures. Although he has made significant contributions to the theory of social control and to an understanding of the stresses and strains peculiar to various social systems, he was unable, given his initial orientation, to advance the theory of social conflict or even to see its general theoretical importance.

That Parsons' orientation in this respect is by no means an exception in the present generation of sociologists becomes evident when we compare his work with that of a writer who is in most respects totally at variance with Parsons' theoretical orientation: George A. Lundberg. In Lundberg's main theoretical work, *The Foundations of Sociology*,[27] only ten out of the more than five hundred pages are allotted to a subchapter dealing in summary fashion with co-operation, competition and conflict, and conflict is furthermore seen as basically dissociative, since it is characterized by "a suspension of communication between the opposing parties." To Lundberg, communication is the essence of the social process and since "abstinence from communication is the essence of conflict situations," conflict must be a purely dysfunctional phenomenon. Lundberg's whole system is oriented toward adjustment. Sociology is explicitly defined as dealing with "the communicable adjustment technics which human groups have developed." By "adjustment" Lundberg means the situation in which the activities of an organism come to rest in equilibrium, and equilibrium in turn is referred to as the "normal" in any social situation. Given these definitional premises, it is readily apparent that Lundberg can see in conflict only a negative and dissociative phenomenon.

Turning to another sociologist of note, we find that the avoidance of conflict (defined as a "social disease") and the promotion of "equilibrium" or a "state of collaboration" (defined as "social health") constitute the main programmatic orientation of Elton Mayo and his school of industrial sociology. As one of the most prominent of the members of the school, F. J. Roethlisberger, poses the problem: "How can a comfortable working equilibrium be maintained between the various social groups in an industrial enterprise such that no one group in the organization will separate itself out in opposition to the remainder?"[28] Mayo's trained incapacity to understand conflicts of interest is evident in all his writings.

All of Mayo's research was carried out with the permission and collaboration of management. It was conducted to help management solve its problems. To Mayo, management embodied the central purposes of society, and with this initial orientation he never considered the possibility that an industrial system might contain conflicting interests, as distinct from different attitudes or "logics."

Similar conclusions result from examination of Lloyd Warner's treatment of social conflict. We are struck here again by the overwhelmingly negative connotations of social conflict. Although individual competition is indeed seen as the very warp of the American democratic structure (of which the social class system is the woof),[29] social conflict—especially class conflict—is viewed as destroying stability and endangering the structure of American society. While Lloyd Warner differs from Elton Mayo in that he has treated one form of social conflict in detail,[30] yet, in viewing social conflict as an exclusively dissociating, corroding, and disruptive phenomenon, he fully agrees with Mayo's orientation.

An anthropological bias in Warner's work toward stability,

harmony and integration of structure, makes conflict exclusively a dissociative and disintegrative phenomenon. "Class analysis," as practiced by Warner and his associates, consists of the identification of various layers of people within a community who have similar social positions and ranking and who associate on intimate terms. The dimension of differential power, differential life chances and differential interests among the members of the community are almost completely ignored, and thereby the emphasis is shifted from questions about conflict or potential conflict to questions about belongingness. When conflict is treated at all, it is treated as a pathological condition which upsets the normal state of community equilibrium.

The last writer we have chosen to discuss, Kurt Lewin, has a somewhat more complex orientation. Centering his interest on the analysis of the life processes of small groups, Kurt Lewin seems to have developed a strangely contradictory attitude toward group conflict. On the one hand, when discussing the situation of minority groups such as the Jews, Lewin voiced the need for a militant affirmation of group identity as the only means for survival and for rejection of attack from the surrounding world. For Jews, as for all underprivileged groups, Lewin felt that "only the efforts of the group itself will achieve the emancipation of the group."[31] Lewin here stood for a militant position emphasizing the need to engage resolutely in conflict activity in order to maintain and insure the existence of the group.

On the other hand, only a few years after these militant articles were written, a distinctly different strain appears in Lewin's work. He is still concerned with conflicts, but with avoiding them, rather than fighting them out. In this new context it is taken for granted that social conflicts are dysfunctional and disintegrating and that the social scientist must concern himself with their reduction. "On whatever unit of group life we focus," Lewin recognized, "whether we think of nations and international politics; of economic life, . . . of race or religious groups, . . . of the factory and the relations between top management and the worker, . . . we find a complicated network of . . . conflicting interests."[32] But these conflicts are now discussed exclusively with a view to their avoidance through "social management." "The research need for social practice can best be characterized as research for social management or social engineering."[33]

It is significant that, to our knowledge, Lewin's earlier emphasis on the positive functions of conflict has not been pursued by his disciples, whereas these men have pushed his emphasis on dysfunctional aspects of conflict behavior much farther than he ever did. The avoidance of conflict is indeed the main content of what has now been designated by the ambiguous term "group skills." The general orientation of the group of Lewin's former students now working at the Research Center for Group Dynamics and at the Bethel Workshop is that conflict is a dysfunctional social phenomenon. Given this general orientation, these researchers are sensitized to the emotional factors which block understanding and communication and they tend to ignore the realistic conflicts which might underlie the "blocked understanding."

III

Our discussion of several representative sociologists of the present generation has shown these men to be less concerned with the sociological analysis of conflict than were the fathers of American sociology. We found that, where such concern does exist, it is directed primarily toward the reduction of conflict. Far from viewing conflict as possibly a necessary and positive part of all social relationships, these sociologists tend to regard it only as a disruptive phenomenon. The prevailing tendency of the thinkers we have rapidly passed in review, is to find "Roads of Agreement" and mutual adjustment through reduction of conflict.

Elsewhere we have discussed in detail some of the reasons for the shifts in the focus of attention and in the evaluation of the problem area with which we are concerned. Here we may only list a few of the factors which seem of relevance, without being able to adduce the necessary proofs of our contention.

Most important, perhaps, is the change that has taken place in the last few decades in the position of the sociologist. The rise of applied social science in this period and the concomitant opening up of opportunities for sociologists to affiliate themselves with extra-academic organizations ranks first in this respect. Whereas in the earlier period sociology was almost completely an academic discipline, the last decades have witnessed the rise of applied sociology and the utilization of the research findings and research personnel of sociology by various public and private bureaucracies. As American sociologists have increasingly turned from "pure" academic research, in which they usually formulated their own problems, to applied research for public and private bureaucracies, they have relinquished to a large extent the freedom to choose their own problems, substituting the problems of their clients for those which might have interested them on purely theoretical grounds.

To the extent that the sociologist works within a business or governmental framework, a change in audience as well as a change in the relation between the sociologist and the audience occurs. The earlier audience, to be sure, influenced the self-image of the sociologists; it provided, perhaps, a market for his books, but it had no way of influencing directly the problem choice he was making; the new audience, on the contrary, is often not only an audience but also an employer. Two consequences follow from this: (1) the sociologist who affiliates himself with public or private bureaucracies will be expected to deal with problems that the decision-makers pose for him; and (2) those problems are likely to concern primarily, as Merton and Lerner have argued, "the preservation of existing institutional arrangements."[34]

The decision-makers are engaged in maintaining and, if possible, strengthening the organizational structures through and in which they exercise power and influence. Whatever conflicts occur within these structures will appear to them to be dysfunctional. Firmly wedded to the existing order by interest and sentiment, the decision-maker tends to view departures from this order as the result of psychological malfunctioning, and to explain conflict behavior as the result of such psychological factors. He will therefore be more likely to concern himself with "tensions" or with "stresses" and "strains" than with those aspects of conflict behavior that might indicate pressures for changing basic institutional arrangements. Also, decision-makers are more likely to consider the dysfunctions of conflict for the total structure, without giving attention to the functions of conflict for particular groups or strata within it.

We have had occasion to encounter similar orientations among sociologists such as Mayo. We do not assert that these men simply took over the views of the decision-makers under whose auspices they pursued their studies; but we hope to have shown that they accepted the decision-makers' choice of problems and that they shared their perspectives regarding conflict phenomena.

Yet this is not sufficient to explain why the majority of present-day sociologists who are not working in applied fields have discarded concern with conflict. Lacking space for full elaboration, we might mention here only the disappearance in the last few decades of the autonomous reform audience that characterized the earlier period; the influence of foundation-sponsored research with the marked reluctance of foundations to sponsor research which might be said to foster reform activities; what might be loosely called the general political atmosphere in a period of the Cold War, as well as the fear of social conflict and the call to unity which seems to pervade much of the current intellectual trends.

The neglect of the study of social conflict and more specifically the neglect of the study of its functions, as distinct from its dysfunctions, can be accounted for to a large extent by the changing roles of American sociologists in recent decades. With the shift from a reform-minded public to an audience of stability-minded administrators and bureaucrats, with the shift of many sociologists from academic and scientific to extra-academic and technical roles, we noted a decreasing concern with the theory of conflict and a tendency to replace analysis of conflict by the study of "tensions," "strains," and psychological malfunctioning.

While early American sociologists addressed themselves primarily to an audience of conflict-oriented groups—lawyers, reformers, radicals, politicians—later American sociologists have found their audience largely among groups and professions concerned with the strengthening of common values and the minimizing of group conflict: social workers, mental health experts, religious leaders, educators, as well as administrators, public and private. The relative weakness of reform movements in the later period and the rise of bureaucratic structures requiring the services of social scientists in the task of administration have helped to bring about this shift in audience. Accompanying this shift, the self-image of many a sociologist has changed from that of a self-conscious advocate of reform to that of a "trouble shooter" and expert in human relations.

Contemporary sociologists have tended to focus on certain aspects of social behavior while neglecting others which may be of equal theoretical importance. The following chapters take up one of these neglected aspects of sociological theory by centering attention upon a series of propositions concerning the functions of social conflict.

IV

A possible procedure for the consolidation of a theory of social conflict would be to isolate some of the central conceptions from the "classical" sociological literature and use them as a springboard for further clarification, linking them up with available research findings and relevant theoretical material. This procedure has the advantage of forcing close attention to the theoretical achievements of an earlier generation of sociologists and of requiring at the same time careful perusal of subsequent writings in an effort to arrive at more adequate respecifications of the initial propositions.

But this procedure was not adopted; it was decided instead to derive the propositions that follow solely from the classical work of Georg Simmel, *Conflict*.[35]

The reason for so confining our primary source is in part a purely pragmatic one. It seemed more convenient, for purposes of exposition, to follow an author with a consistent general orientation rather than to shift between writers whose orientations may be divergent. But a more important reason is that Simmel's essay on conflict, rooted as it is in his general commitment to the analysis of social phenomena in terms of interactive processes, is the most fruitful among general discussions of social conflict.

This anchoring of our study upon the work of Simmel does not imply, of course, that we consider all his contributions to be the present frontier of speculation and thinking about conflict. As our discussion proceeds, it will become evident that some of his formulations are relatively crude if measured against subsequent work, both theoretical and empirical. In a number of instances the frontier of knowledge about conflict has moved beyond the point reached by Simmel.

For our purposes it is not necessary to consider all the intricacies of Simmel's thought; the propositions to be discussed do not even exhaust the content of his work on conflict. Rather we intended to identify in Simmel's extensive account only those propositions that seem most relevant for a contemporary theory of the functions of social conflict. This is not a study in the history of ideas; we are not interested here in the analysis of past sociological writings, but in the uses of the inheritance. Sociological theorizing must continuously draw upon those past contributions that provide clues for the further extension of knowledge, and for this purpose only certain parts of the work of a classical theorist are likely to be of use. This Simmel himself well knew when he wrote in his diary: "I know that I will die without intellectual heirs—and that is as it should be. My legacy will be as it were in cash, distributed to many heirs, each transforming his part into use conforming to his own nature: a use that will no longer reveal its indebtedness to this heritage."[36]

The proclivity of Simmel for relating hitherto unconnected, yet perceptive insights often has been noted. José Ortega y Gasset well characterized the peculiarity of Simmel's thought when he wrote of him: "That acute mind—a sort of philosophical squirrel —never considered his subject a problem in itself, but instead took it as a platform upon which to execute his marvelous analytical exercises."[37] Simmel's ideas are not derived from a general theoretical framework, as are those of Freud or Marx. Thus, although a theory can be found *in nuce* in Simmel's work, this theory can be more effectively stated by incorporating into it the central ideas on this matter of other sociologists.

In examining the propositions derived from Simmel, we will confront them with relevant ideas of other social theorists and with evidence that tends to illustrate, modify or invalidate them. Our concern will be to clarify those propositions, to examine the internal consistency of each as well as the logical interrelation of all. We are not primarily concerned with verification; this would be possible only by testing the theory through systematic empirical research.

Simmel's essay, to which we now turn, is informed by the central thesis that "conflict is a form of socialization." This means essentially that, to paraphrase the opening pages of Simmel's essay, no group can be entirely harmonious, for it would then be devoid of process and structure. Groups require disharmony as well as harmony, dissociation as well as association; and conflicts within them are by no means altogether disruptive factors. Group formation is the result of both types of processes. The belief that one process tears down what the other builds up, so that what finally remains is the result of subtracting the one from the other, is based on a misconception. On the contrary, both "positive" and "negative" factors build group relations. Conflict as well as co-operation has social functions. Far from being necessarily dysfunctional, a certain degree of conflict is an essential element in group formation and the persistence of group life.

The following propositions derive from this basic view of the functions of social conflict.

CHAPTER II

CONFLICT AND
GROUP BOUNDARIES

PROPOSITION I:

Group-Binding Functions of Conflict

"A certain amount of discord, inner divergence and outer controversy, is organically tied up with the very elements that ultimately hold the group together . . . the positive and integrating role of antagonism is shown in structures which stand out by the sharpness and carefully preserved purity of their social divisions and gradations. Thus, the Hindu social system rests not only on the hierarchy, but also directly on the mutual repulsion, of the castes. Hostilities not only prevent boundaries within the group from gradually disappearing . . . often they provide classes and individuals with reciprocal positions which they would not find . . . if the causes of hostility were not accompanied by the feeling and the expression of hostility."[1]

A CLARIFICATION IS NECESSARY HERE. Simmel shifts between sociological and psychological statements, as when he passes from discussion of personal autonomy to group autonomy, thus obscuring the fact that although the personality and the social system may be partly homologous and although they interpenetrate, they are by no means identical.[2] Genetic psychology[3] and psychoanalysis have gathered much evidence to suggest that conflict is a most important agent for the establishment of full ego identity and autonomy, i.e., for full differentiation of the personality from the outside world. However, this problem will not be the concern of the present study which intends to deal primarily with the behavior of individuals in groups. For this reason, "feelings of hostility and repulsion" will be discussed only where they are part of a social *pattern*, i.e., where their regular occurrence can be observed. Individual behavior which is merely idiosyncratic has no place in the analysis of structured social systems.

Turning to the sociological content of the proposition, we note that Simmel deals with two related yet distinct phenomena. He holds first that conflict sets boundaries between groups within a social system by strengthening group consciousness and awareness of separateness, thus establishing the identity of groups within the system. And second, he says that reciprocal "repulsions" maintain a total social system by creating a balance between its various groups. For example, conflicts between Indian castes may establish the separateness and distinctiveness of the various castes, but may also insure the stability of the total Indian social structure by bringing about a balance of claims by rival castes. Elsewhere Simmel has stressed even more strongly the group-binding character of conflict.[4]

This insight is, of course, not new. We could quote similar statements from social theorists since antiquity. Writing at the same time as Simmel, William Graham Sumner, in his discussion of in-group and out-group relations, expressed essentially the same idea.[5]

Familiar as this insight is, it is not necessarily incorporated in all contemporary sociological theory. Thus Parsons in his recent work,[6] while stressing that social systems are of the "boundary-maintaining" type, i.e., that they must maintain delimitations between themselves and the environment if they are to keep constancies of pattern, fails to mention conflict in this connection.[7]

This function of conflict in establishing and maintaining group identities has been accorded a certain place in the work of theorists such as Georg Sorel and Karl Marx. Sorel's advocacy of "violence" is to be understood entirely in terms of his awareness of the close relations between conflict and group cohesion.[8] He felt that only if the working class is constantly engaged in war-fare with the middle class can it preserve its distinctive character. Only through and in action can its members become conscious and aware of their class identity. Underlying his insistence that socialists, with whom he identified himself, must oppose humani-tarian moves on the part of the governing classes, is the sociologi-cal dictum that such measures would lead to a decrease in class conflict and hence to a weakening of class identity. For Marx also, classes constitute themselves only through conflict. Indi-viduals may have objective common positions in society, but they become aware of the community of their interests only in and through conflict. "The separate individuals form a class only in so far as they have to carry on a common battle against another class; otherwise they are on hostile terms with each other as competitors."[9]

It seems to be generally accepted by sociologists that the dis-tinction between "ourselves, the we-group, or in-group, and everybody else, or the others-groups, out-groups"[10] is estab-lished in and through conflict. This is not confined to conflict between classes, although class conflicts have appeared as the most convenient illustrations to many observers. Nationality and ethnic conflicts, political conflicts, or conflicts between various strata in bureaucratic structures afford equally relevant examples.

Simmel goes on to say that enmities and reciprocal antagonisms also maintain the total system by establishing a balance between its component parts. This takes place, according to Simmel, be-cause members of the same stratum or caste are drawn together in a solidarity resulting from their common enmity to and re-jection of members of other strata or castes. In this way, a hier-archy of positions is maintained because of the aversion that the various members of the subgroups within the total society have for each other.

This view requires qualification. As has been pointed out,[11] out-groups, far from necessarily constituting targets of hostility, can also, under certain conditions, become positive references to the in-group. The out-group may be emulated as well as resented. Emulation is minimized only under certain conditions, for example, in a strict caste system such as the Indian in which there is no emphasis on social mobility and in which caste position is legitimized by religous beliefs.[12] Although lower castes will look upon higher castes as their hierarchical superiors, they will not be likely to desire to move out of their own lower caste situation or to emulate the behavior of the higher caste.[13]

The situation is fundamentally different in a class system that provides a substantial degree of social mobility. It remains true that status groups within the American system often regard each other with invidious or hostile feelings. It is also true that the structure of the system is maintained partly by these reciprocal antagonisms which preserve gradations of status. Nevertheless, members of the lower strata often emulate the higher, and aspire to membership in higher strata. Thus, voluntary associations in Yankee City[14] helped to organize the antagonisms of various "classes" to each other, but at the same time they functioned to "organize and regulate upward mobility." In societies in which upward social mobility is institutionalized, in which achieved rather than ascribed status dominates, hostility between various strata is mingled with a strong positive attraction to those higher in the social hierarchy, who provide some models of behavior. If there were no antagonisms, status groups would dissolve since boundaries between them and the outside would disappear; but these boundaries are kept fluid by the very fact that upward social mobility is the cultural ideal of such societies.

It is for this reason that feelings of interclass hostility typical in an open class system, as distinct from a caste system, are often likely to turn into *ressentiment*.[15] They do not indicate genuine rejection of the values or groups against which these negative feelings are directed, but rather a "sour-grapes" attitude: that which is condemned is secretly craved.

It should be noted that Simmel does not explicitly distinguish between feelings of hostility and the actual acting out of these feelings. There is an evident difference between the Indian caste system in which feelings of antagonism do not lead to open conflict and the American class system in which conflict (e.g., between management and labor) is a frequent and expected occurrence. Unequal distributions of privileges and rights may lead to sentiments of hostility, but they do not necessarily lead to conflict. A distinction between conflict and hostile sentiments is essential. Conflict, as distinct from hostile attitudes or sentiments, always takes place in interaction between two or more persons. Hostile attitudes are predispositions to engage in conflict behavior; conflict, on the contrary, is always a *trans*-action.[16]

Whether feelings of hostility lead to conflict behavior depends in part on whether or not the unequal distribution of rights is considered legitimate. In the classical Indian caste system, intercaste conflict was rare because lower and higher castes alike accepted the caste distinctions.[17] *Legitimacy* is a crucial intervening variable without which it is impossible to predict whether feelings of hostility arising out of an unequal distribution of privileges and rights will actually lead to conflict.

Before a social conflict between negatively and positively privileged groups can take place, before hostile attitudes are turned into social action, the negatively privileged group must first develop the awareness that it is, indeed, negatively privileged. It must come to believe that it is being denied rights to which it is entitled. It must reject any justification for the existing distribution of rights and privileges. Shifts in the degree of acceptance of a given distribution of power, wealth or status are closely connected with shifts in the selection of reference groups in varying social situations. In the Indian case discussed above, it would seem that changes in economic institutions (for example, from agriculture to industry, and concomitant opening of opportunities for mobility) have been instrumental in inducing the negatively privileged groups to change their definitions of self and others.

For our purposes, it need only be noted that when a social structure is no longer considered legitimate, individuals with similar objective positions will come, through conflict, to constitute themselves into self-conscious groups with common interests.[18] This process of group formation will concern us further in the discussion of later propositions.

Social structures differ as to the degree of conflict which they tolerate. As will be seen in the next proposition, Simmel implies that where the structure inhibits the expression and acting out of hostile feelings, substitute mechanisms for the venting of such feelings can be expected to exist.

We can now rephrase Simmel's proposition:

Conflict serves to establish and maintain the identity and boundary lines of societies and groups.

Conflict with other groups contributes to the establishment and reaffirmation of the identity of the group and maintains its boundaries against the surrounding social world.

Patterned enmities and reciprocal antagonisms conserve social divisions and systems of stratification. Such patterned antagonisms prevent the gradual disappearance of boundaries between the subgroups of a social system and they assign position to the various subsystems within a total system.

In social structures providing a substantial amount of mobility, attraction of the lower strata by the higher, as well as mutual hostility between the strata, is likely to occur. Hostile feelings of the lower strata in this case frequently take the form of *ressentiment* in which hostility is mingled with attraction. Such structures will tend to provide many occasions for conflict since, as will be discussed later, frequency of occasions for conflict varies positively with the closeness of relations.

A distinction has to be made between conflict and hostile or antagonistic attitudes. Social conflict always denotes social interaction, whereas attitudes or sentiments are predispositions to engage in action. Such predispositions do not necessarily eventuate in conflict; the degree and kind of legitimation of power and status systems are crucial intervening variables affecting the occurrence of conflict.

CHAPTER III

HOSTILITY AND TENSIONS
IN CONFLICT RELATIONSHIPS

PROPOSITION 2:

Group-Preserving Functions of Conflict and
the Significance of Safety-Valve Institutions

". . . the opposition of a member to an associate is no purely negative social factor, if only because such opposition is often the only means for making life with actually unbearable people at least possible. If we did not even have the power and the right to rebel against tyranny, arbitrariness, moodiness, tactlessness, we could not bear to have any relation to people from whose characters we thus suffer. We would feel pushed to take desperate steps—and these, indeed, would end the relation but do *not*, perhaps, constitute 'conflict.' Not only because of the fact that . . . oppression usually increases if it is suffered calmly and without protest, but also because opposition gives us inner satisfaction, distraction, relief. . . . Our opposition makes us feel that we are not completely victims of the circumstances."[1]

SIMMEL HERE ASSERTS that the expression of hostility in conflict serves positive functions insofar as it permits the maintenance of relationships under conditions of stress, thus preventing group dissolution through the withdrawal of hostile participants.

Conflict is thus seen as performing group-maintaining functions insofar as it regulates systems of relationships. It "clears the air," i.e., it eliminates the accumulation of blocked and balked hostile dispositions by allowing their free behavioral expression. Simmel

[39]

echoes Shakespeare's King John: "So foul a sky clears not without a storm."

At first view, it would appear that Simmel, contrary to his general tendency, considers only the effect of conflict on one part—the aggrieved—without considering the reciprocal response. But in fact his examination of the "release" functions of conflict for aggrieved individuals or groups concerns him only insofar as such "release" allows the maintenance of the relationship, i.e., of the interactive pattern.

However, Simmel's failure, already noted earlier, to distinguish between conflict behavior and hostile feelings again leads to difficulties. Whereas conflict necessarily changes the previous terms of the relationship of the participants, mere hostility has no such necessary effects and may leave the terms of the relationship unchanged.

Turning to the significance of individual release, we note that Simmel was not aware of a problem brought into view by subsequent psychological theorizing. Accumulated hostile or aggressive dispositions may be discharged not only against the original object of hostility, but against substitute objects. Simmel apparently considered only direct conflict with the primary sources of opposition. He also failed to concern himself with the possibility that modes of behavior other than conflict might at least partly perform functions similar to those of conflict.

Writing in Berlin around the turn of the century, Simmel was not yet acquainted with the revolutionary developments in psychology which occurred roughly at the same time in Vienna. Had he been familiar with the then new theory of psychoanalysis, he would have avoided the assumption that feelings of hostility can be acted out in conflict behavior only against the very cause of hostility. He did not conceive of the possibilities that in cases in which conflict behavior against the original object is blocked (1) hostile feelings may be deflected upon substitute objects and that (2) substitute satisfaction may be attained through mere tension release. In both cases the continuance of the original relationship may be facilitated.

In order to examine the present proposition it is necessary, then, to maintain the first distinction between feelings of hostility and their behavioral manifestations. Moreover, the relevant expression of these feelings in behavior are of at least three possible kinds: (1) direct expression of hostility against the person or group which is the source of frustration, (2) displacement of such hostile behavior onto substitute objects, and (3) tension-release activity which provides satisfaction in itself without need for object or object substitute.

Simmel may be said to advance a "safety-valve theory" of conflict. Conflict serves as an outlet for the release of hostilities which, were no such outlet provided, would sunder the relation between the antagonists.

The German ethnologist Heinrich Schurtz[2] coined the word *Ventilsitten* for those mores and institutions in primitive societies that provide institutionalized outlets for hostilities and drives ordinarily suppressed by the group. Orgiastic feasts in which ordinary rules of sexual behavior and avoidance can safely be infringed afford a convenient example. Such outlets, as the German sociologist Vierkandt has pointed out, serve as a kind of river bed for repressed drives and thus preserve the rest of social life from their destructive impact.[3]

Yet, the concept of "safety valve," if understood in terms of the distinctions which we have just made, is ambiguous. Attack against substitute objects or abreaction of hostile energies in other types of activities may also be said to fulfill safety-valve functions. Like Simmel, both Schurtz and Vierkandt fail to distinguish between *Ventilsitten*, which provide a socially sanctioned framework for carrying out conflict without leading to consequences that disrupt relationships within a group, and those safety-valve institutions which serve to divert hostility onto substitute objects or which function as channels for cathartic release.

Pertinent illustrations are more accessible from nonliterate societies, possibly because anthropologists have concerned themselves with this problem more systematically than have students of Western society, although the latter also have provided us with some relevant data. An illustration of safety-valve mores which provide a sanctioned outlet for hostilities against the *original* object is supplied by the institution of the duel both in Europe and in nonliterate societies. Dueling brings potentially disruptive aggressive self-help under social control and constitutes a direct outlet for hostilities between members of the society. The socially controlled conflict "clears the air" between the participants and allows a resumption of their relationships. If one of the participants is killed, his kin and friends are assumed not to continue the hostility against his adversary: the affair is then "socially closed" and relations can resume.

Socially approved, controlled and limited acts of revenge fall into the same category.

> In an Australian tribe when one man has committed an offense against another, the latter is permitted by public opinion . . . to throw a certain number of spears or boomerangs at the former or in some instances to spear him in the thigh. After he has been given such satisfaction he may no longer harbor ill feelings against the offender. In many preliterate societies, the killing of an individual entitles the group to which he belongs to obtain satisfaction by killing the offender or some member of his group. In regulated vengeance the offending group must submit to this as an act of justice and must not attempt further retaliation. Those who have received such satisfaction are felt to have no further grounds for ill feelings.[4]

In both instances hostile feelings are allowed socially sanctioned expression against the adversary.

Consider, on the other hand, such institutions as witchcraft. Many observers have pointed out that though witchcraft is indeed often used as a means of revenge against an object of hostility, the voluminous literature on witchcraft abounds with cases in which those accused of witchcraft had not in any way harmed their accusers or aroused hostility, but were singled out as a means for the release of hostility which could not be expressed safely against the original object.

In his study on Navaho witchcraft, Clyde Kluckhohn describes witchcraft as an institution permitting not only direct aggression, but also displacement of hostility onto substitute objects. "A latent function of the corpus of witchcraft for individuals is that of providing a socially recognized channel for the expression of the culturally disallowed." "Witchcraft beliefs and practices allow the expression of direct and displaced antagonism." "If myths and rituals provide the principal means of sublimating the Navaho individual's anti-social tendencies, witchcraft provides the principally socially understood means of expressing them." "Witchcraft channels the displacement of aggression, facilitating emotional adjustment with a minimum of disturbance of social relationships."[5]

There are cases in which hostility is indeed expressed against the original object, but it may be expressed indirectly and even unwittingly. Freud's discussion of the function of wit in aggression informs this distinction. "Wit permits us to make our enemy ridiculous through that which we could not utter loudly or consciously on account of existing hindrances." "Wit is used with special preference as a weapon of attack or criticism of superiors who claim to be in authority. Wit then serves as a resistance against such authority and as an escape from its pressures."[6] Freud refers to the displacement of the *means* of expressing hostility. He makes it clear that the positive function for the individual which Simmel imputes to conflict may also be accomplished by indirect means, of which wit is only one.[7]

Since displaced means such as wit may not bring about a change in the relations between one person and another, especially if the target of the aggressive wit is not aware of the source and intention of the witticism, they may afford expression to the weaker member without changing the terms of the relationship. Such opposition frequently shades into a simple substitute pleasure which is the functional equivalent of mere tension release. The outcrop of political jokes in totalitarian countries bears witness to this, as does the statement attributed to Goebbels that the Nazi regime actually welcomed political jokes since they provided harmless outlets for hostilities.

Theatre and other forms of entertainment may provide similar *displaced means* for the expression of opposition against the original source of hostility. In Bali,[8] where the social structure is highly stratified and rigid, great attention being paid to the etiquette of rank and status, the theatre specializes in parodies of rank. These "skits on status" consist, for example, of dances in which people stand on their heads with feet doing duty as hands and with masks set on their pubes. "This freedom of theatrical caricature . . . concentrates on the points of stress in the system, and so provides continual release in laughter." It is suggested that the Balinese theatre drains off latent hostilities which are bred in this rigidly stratified society and thereby allows its continued functioning—although the authors do not produce evidence sufficient to demonstrate this.

In these and similar cases we note that though hostility may be expressed, the relationship as such remains unchanged. Whereas conflict changes the terms of the interaction, mere expression of hostile feelings does not. Thus expression, as distinct from conflict, may be welcomed by the powers that be.

The distinction which we introduced between displacement of means and displacement of object is of great sociological significance, for in the case of displacement of means (as through wit, theatre, etc.), no conflict is carried out. In aggression against substitute objects, however (as in witchcraft or any form of scapegoating), though the original relationship is safeguarded by channeling aggression away from it, a new conflict situation with the substitute object is called into being. This second type of relationship involves conditions of "unrealistic" conflict which we will discuss in the next proposition.

Institutions which channel the expression of hostile feelings are, of course, not limited to preliterate societies. Stimulated by the Freudian hypothesis of "a primary hostility of men towards one another,"[9] many observers have pointed to the function of mass culture as a general means of "safe" release of aggressive drives which are tabooed in other social contexts.[10] The great popularity of boxing and wrestling matches on television may be partly accounted for by the vicarious participation in conflict provided the onlooker who identifies with his hero "hitting the other fellow in the snout." Contemporary mass culture serves as one means of release from frustrations and allows the vicarious expression of strongly tabooed hostile impulses. As Herta Herzog notes in her study of "Psychological Gratifications in Daytime Radio Listening," "some listeners seem to enjoy the serials merely as a means of emotional release. They like 'the chance to cry' which the serials provide. . . . The opportunity for expressing aggressiveness is also a source of satisfaction."[11]

Several of these examples suggest the hypothesis that the need for safety-valve institutions increases with the rigidity of the social structure, that is, with the degree to which the social system disallows expression of antagonistic claims where they occur.[12] A number of intervening variables, such as the general value orientation, the level of security, etc., would have to be considered. The topic will be discussed further in later propositions.

The well-known "scapegoating" mechanism operative in group conflict is relevant in this context. Discussion of the vast literature that has appeared in recent years on this and other aspects of prejudice[13] cannot be attempted here. Some aspects of "scapegoating" will be discussed in the next proposition and again in a later part of this work. It is sufficient to say at this point that prejudice studies have focused attention almost exclusively on the personality of the prejudiced—possibly because modern research methods lend themselves better to such use—while slighting the social functions of prejudice. Racial and religious prejudice, by channeling hostilities onto powerless targets, may contribute as much to the stability of existing social structures as the safety-valve institutions discussed above.[14]

All this raises a problem previously alluded to, of central importance for the theory of conflict: an institution which serves to channel hostility and to prevent release against the original object, thereby maintaining the structure of the social system, may also have serious dysfunctions for either the social system or the actor, or both. As Clyde Kluckhohn notes: *"Witchcraft has its cost for the individual and for the group."*[15]

The availability of safety-valve institutions[16] leads to a displacement of goal in the actor: he need no longer aim at reaching a solution of the unsatisfactory situation, but merely at releasing the tension which arose from it. In this way the unsatisfactory situation will remain unaltered or become intensified. The next proposition will attempt to show that whether or not the goal is displaced is an important variable in the theory of conflict.

Psychologists have shown experimentally that overt aggression is more satisfying than nonovert aggression;[17] similarly, there is at least a presumption that conflict carried out directly against the object may prove to be less dysfunctional for the social system than channeling of aggressiveness through safety-valve institutions.

Institutions which offer substitute channels for the release of aggressiveness may be dysfunctional for the social system in the same way as neurotic symptoms are dysfunctional for the personality system. Neurotic symptoms are a result of repression while at the same time they provide partial satisfaction of the repressed drives. The dammed-up drives "find other ways out from the unconscious. . . . What results is a *symptom* and consequently in its essence a *substitutive satisfaction*. . . . The symptom cannot entirely escape from the repressive force of the ego and must therefore submit to modifications and displacements. . . . Thus symptoms are in the nature of compromise-formations between the repressed . . . instincts and the repressive ego . . . ; they represent a wish fulfillment for both partners to the conflict simultaneously, but one which is incomplete for both of them."[18] "In the unconscious the repressed idea remains capable of action and must therefore have retained its cathexis."[19]

Freud's method of defining the neurotic symptom and its function might be usefully applied here: (1) His heuristic principle of interaction between the id which desires satisfaction and the ego which seeks to repress this desire might be applied to the interaction between the person who seeks satisfaction and the institutions which serve to block it and substitute for it. We may paraphrase Freud's observation and say that *safety-valve institutions are positively functional for both individual and social structure, but incompletely functional for both of them.*[20] (2) Since the release is incomplete for the individual, the idea which is wholly or partially repressed "remains capable of action."

Damming up of unrelieved or only partially relieved tensions, instead of permitting adjustment to changed conditions, leads to rigidity in the structure and creates potentialities for disruptive explosion.

Moreover, a contemporary psychoanalyst has this to say concerning the "wholesome effect" of mere tension release:

> Previously "abreaction" was considered the therapeutically decisive factor. And it is true that a liberation of hitherto blocked emotions takes place. . . . However, no true and permanent dissolution of the defense struggle can be achieved in this way. . . . Not only must previously bound energies become free in a single act, but newly produced instinctual tension must permanently be enabled to get discharge as well.[21]

If, as Simmel implies, "conflict clears the air," institutions that merely serve abreaction of feelings of hostility, thus leaving the terms of the relationship unchanged, may function as lightning rods but they cannot prevent a recurrent gathering of clouds, i.e., a new accumulation of tension.

However, there may be between group members relationships so tenuous that they cannot withstand the impact of conflict and require substitutes in order to endure. This subject will be taken up later.

With the above discussion in mind, we may now reformulate the present proposition:

(1) Conflict is not always dysfunctional for the relationship within which it occurs; often conflict is necessary to maintain such a relationship. Without ways to vent hostility toward each other, and to express dissent, group members might feel completely crushed and might react by withdrawal. By setting free

pent-up feelings of hostility, conflicts serve to maintain a relationship.

(2) Social systems provide for specific institutions which serve to drain off hostile and aggressive sentiments. These safety-valve institutions help to maintain the system by preventing otherwise probable conflict or by reducing its disruptive effects. They provide substitute objects upon which to displace hostile sentiments, as well as means of abreaction. Through these safety valves, hostility is prevented from turning against its original object. But such displacements also involve costs both for the social system and for the individual: reduced pressure for modifying the system to meet changing conditions, as well as dammed-up tension in the individual, creating potentialities for disruptive explosion.

Release of hostile sentiments upon a substitute object (as distinct from simple symbolic expression) creates a new conflict situation with that object. The distinction between such "unrealistic conflict" and "realistic conflict" will be developed in the next proposition.

PROPOSITION 3:

Realistic and Nonrealistic Conflict

"If the conflict is caused by an object, by the will to have or control something, by rage or revenge . . . it is qualified by the fact that, in principle, every end can be attained by more than one means. The desire for possession or subjugation, even for the annihilation of the enemy, can be satisfied through combinations and events other than fight. Where conflict is merely a means determined by a superior purpose, there is no reason to restrict or even avoid it, provided it can be replaced by other measures which have the same promise of success. Where, on the other hand, it is exclusively determined by subjective feelings, where there are inner energies which *can* be satisfied only through fight, its substitution by other means is impossible; it is its own purpose and content. . . ."[22]

[48]

Simmel asserts that conflicts occasioned by clashes of interests or clashes of personalities contain an element of limitation insofar as the struggle is only a means toward an end; if the desired result can be attained as well or better by other means, such other means may be employed. In such instances, conflict is only one of several functional alternatives.

There are cases, however, where the conflict arises exclusively from aggressive impulses which seek expression no matter what the object, where in the conflict the choice of object is purely accidental. In such cases, no such limitations exist, since it is not the attainment of a result, but rather the acting out of aggressive energies which occasions the outbreak.

Implicit in this differentiation between conflict as a means and conflict as an end in itself is a criterion by which to distinguish between *realistic* and *nonrealistic* conflict. Conflicts which arise from frustration of specific demands within the relationship and from estimates of gains of the participants, and which are directed at the presumed frustrating object, can be called *realistic conflicts*, insofar as they are means toward a specific result. *Nonrealistic conflicts*, on the other hand, although still involving interaction between two or more persons, are not occasioned by the rival ends of the antagonists, but by the need for tension release of at least one of them. In this case the choice of antagonists depends on determinants not directly related to a contentious issue and is not oriented toward the attainment of specific results.

Else Frenkel-Brunswick, discussing the "ethnocentric personality," makes precisely this point when she writes: "Even his hate is mobile and can be directed from one object to another."[23] John Dewey's dictum, "men do not shoot because targets exist, but they set up targets in order that throwing and shooting may be more effective and significant,"[24] applies to this type of nonrealistic conflict.

Thus anti-Semitism, except where it is caused by conflicts of interests or values between the Jewish and other groups or individuals, will be called nonrealistic insofar as it is primarily a response to frustrations in which the object appears suitable for a release of aggressiveness. Whether this object be Jews, Negroes, or some other group is of secondary importance to the aggressor.[25]

Nonrealistic conflict, occasioned by the need for release of aggressive tension in one or more of the interacting persons, is less "stable" than realistic conflict. The underlying aggressiveness can more easily be led into other channels, precisely because it is not directly bound to the object, which has become a target by "situational accident." It is likely to manifest itself in different ways if the particular object is no longer available.

Realistic conflict, on the other hand, will cease if the actor can find equally satisfying alternative ways to achieve his end.[26] In realistic conflict, there exist *functional alternatives as to means*. Means other than conflict, depending on assessments of their efficacy, are always potentially available to the participants. In addition, it should be noted that in realistic conflicts there are also possibilities of choice between various forms of contention, such choice depending similarly on an assessment of their instrumental adequacy. In nonrealistic conflict, on the other hand, there exist only *functional alternatives as to objects*.

A distinction along these lines should help to avoid the fallacy of trying to explain the social phenomena of realistic conflict entirely in terms of "tension release." For example, a worker engaged in strike activity in order to increase his wages, his status or the power of his union, and one who releases aggression against the boss because he perceives him as an oedipal figure, are dissimilar social types. Displaced father hatred may attach itself to any suitable object—boss, policeman or staff sergeant. The economic fight of workers against the boss, on the other hand, is based on their particular positions and roles in the economic and political system. They can choose to give up the conflict and reach accommodation if it seems opportune to do so; they can also choose means of carrying it out other than strikes, such as collective bargaining, negotiations, slowdowns, etc.

Antagonistic action on the part of labor against management, or vice versa, can be said to be realistic insofar as it is a means for obtaining results (higher status, more power, greater economic returns); if the aim of labor or management is the achievement of these results and not the mere expression of diffuse hostilities, such conflict is less likely to take place whenever alternative means will help to attain the goal.

Such a distinction might serve to inform discussions of social control and social deviance. A social deviant need not be "irrational," or devoid of reality orientation, as much theorizing has tacitly assumed. The deviant behavior which Merton analyzes in "Social Structure and Anomie,"[27] insofar as it represents efforts to reach culturally prescribed goals through culturally tabooed means, would constitute one of the variants of realistic struggle. If the type of deviants involved here should find at their disposal legitimate means to attain the same goal, they are less likely to engage in deviant behavior. Deviance, in this case, is more nearly instrumental than expressive. Other types of deviance, however, may serve to release tension accumulated during the socialization process and through frustration and deprivations in adult roles. In these cases the deviant values the aggressive behavior in itself; the object against which the act is directed is of secondary import. Fulfillment of the tensional need is primary, and hence the act does not serve as a means to the attainment of a specific result. In such cases, there is less likely to be a weighing of peaceful against aggressive means, since it is precisely in the aggressive means and not in the result that satisfaction is sought.[28]

Failure to make the proposed distinction accounts for much of the confusion in current research on "tensions" and "aggression."[29] Knowledge gained from the study of nonrealistic conflict is being applied to the field of international relations, overlooking the fact that conflicts in this field are primarily realistic conflicts of 'power, interests or values and that the nonrealistic elements which may be intermingled in the struggle are contingent and play, at best, a reinforcing role.[30] As Alvin Johnson has said, "It is commonly assumed that antipathies between people . . . have played a large part in the causation of war. History offers singularly little evidence upon which such a view can be based. . . . Such antipathies . . . appear rather to be the result than a

[51]

cause of war."[31] The psychologist who studies displacement mechanisms is rightly concerned primarily with the personality of the prejudiced individual, while the target of the aggressive drive concerns him only incidentally. But in the study of a conflict situation in which the *interaction* is of major concern, the sociologist must investigate the conflict relationship and the exclusive values or divergent interests which the contenders pursue.[32] There is no justification for *a priori* regarding claims in a conflict situation as equivalent to the statement that "the center of the earth is made of jam."[33] Thus a sociological study of international politics, although it may legitimately concern itself with tensions arising from various frustrations within national social systems, will not accomplish its main purpose unless it analyzes the realistic conflicts over scarce power around which the patterns of alliance and antagonisms form.

Similarly, the studies in industrial sociology inspired by Elton Mayo show no recognition of the existence of realistic conflict or of its functions. Behavior which is the outcome of a conflict situation is almost exclusively dealt with as nonrealistic behavior. They counterpose a logic of facts, "the logic of cost and the logic of efficiency " (i.e., "facts" which aim at beneficial results for management) to "the logic of sentiments," thus depriving the workers' claims of their realistic basis. "The implication that emerges, whether intended or not, is that managers are guided by a logic of reason whereas workers are largely creatures of feelings and emotions."[34] The emphasis on "sentiments" obscures the existence of realistic conflict. Indeed, these studies show a peculiar lack of sensitivity to struggles over power or pecuniary gains that arise in the factory.

With the possibility of realistic conflict ruled out, the managerial sociologists are naturally led to "wonder what kind of man it must be who can get such an idea into his head" and, instead of directing their attention to the investigation of the conflict situation, they look for "therapeutic measures." Committed to the view that the source of conflict is to be found in sentiments which distort relations rather than in the nature of these social relations themselves, they see all conflict as "social disease" and the lack of conflict as "social health."[35] Their center of attention is neither the source of frustration nor the issue at stake, but the effect of frustration on the individual. In the words of Dale Carnegie, they attempt "to make the other man happy about the thing you suggest" by directing feelings of hostility into "safe" channels.[36] Thus Roethlisberger and Dickson can write with admirable frankness about the counselling system: "This kind of non-authoritative agency serves to control and direct those human processes within the industrial structure which are not adequately controlled by other agencies of management."[37]

The distinction between realistic and nonrealistic conflict involves a conceptual abstraction from concrete reality in which the two types actually may be merged. However, as Max Weber has pointed out, "the construction of a purely rational course of action . . . serves the sociologist as a type. . . . By comparison with this it is possible to understand the ways in which actual action is influenced by irrational factors of all sorts . . . in that they account for the deviation from the line of conduct which would be expected on the hypothesis that the action was purely rational."[38]

Realistic conflict situations may be accompanied, especially where there are no adequate provisions for the carrying out of the struggle, by unrealistic sentiments which are deflected from their source. In concrete social reality an admixture of both "pure" types will be found. Talcott Parsons expressed this very well in his description of the scapegoat mechanism: "Since it would be dangerous and wrong to freely express overt antagonism toward the members of the in-group, it is often psychologically easier to 'displace' the affect onto an out-group in relation to which there *already exists*[39] some basis of antagonism. Scapegoating thus rarely appears without *some*[40] 'reasonable' basis of antagonism in that there is a real conflict of ideals or interests."[41] In other words, one of the sources of unrealistic admixtures in realistic conflicts lies in institutions which define the free expression of overt antagonism as "dangerous and wrong."

The term "realistic conflict" does not necessarily imply that the means adopted are actually adequate for reaching the end in view; the means may merely seem to be adequate to the participants, if only for the reason that they are culturally approved. Workers who go on strike to force the exclusion from the shop of Negro fellow-workers in order to maintain their wage rates are engaged in realistic conflict. But (and this is the essence of Simmel's proposition) if the situation is so changed that other means prove more rewarding with regard to wage rates, the workers are more likely to refrain from discriminatory action. Should they, however, maintain the discriminatory practice although other more effective means to the same end are available, it can be provisionally supposed that nonrealistic elements, such as "prejudice," are being expressed in the conflict.[42]

Perhaps enough has been said to clarify the reasons for distinguishing between realistic and nonrealistic types of conflict.

Each social system contains sources of realistic conflict insofar as people raise conflicting claims to scarce status, power and resources, and adhere to conflicting values. The allocation of status, power and resources, though governed by norms and role allocation systems, will continue to be an object of contention to some degree. Realistic conflicts arise when men clash in the pursuit of claims based on frustration of demands and expectancies of gains.

Nonrealistic conflicts arise from deprivations and frustrations stemming from the socialization process and from later adult role obligations, or they result, as we have seen in the previous proposition, from a conversion of originally realistic antagonism which was disallowed expression. Whereas the first type of conflict takes place with the frustrating agents themselves in expectation of attaining specific results, the second type consists of a release of tension in aggressive action directed against shifting objects. The first type of conflict is viewed by the participants as a means toward the achievement of realistic ends, a means which might be abandoned if other means appear to be more effective for reaching the same end. The second leaves no such choice, since satisfaction is derived from the aggressive act itself.

Realistic conflicts accompanied by emotionally distorted sentiments will be discussed again in the next proposition.

PROPOSITION 4:

Conflict and Hostile Impulses

"Assuming that there indeed exists a formal hostility drive as the counterpart of the need for sympathy. . . . No matter how much psychological autonomy one may be willing to grant the antagonistic drive, this autonomy is not enough to account for all phenomena involving hostility. . . . Love and hate . . . seem to need some appealing structure of their objects with whose cooperation alone they yield the total phenomena that go by their name. . . . It seems probable to me that . . . the hostility drive merely adds itself as a reinforcement . . . to controversies which are due to concrete causes. . . . It is *expedient* to hate the adversary with whom one fights, just as it is expedient to love a person whom one is tied to."[43]

In this proposition, Simmel makes two main points:
(1) Feelings of hostility arise in the interplay between an "impulse of hostility" and an opposing object.
(2) The analysis of conflict situations is not exhausted by reference to psychic motivations; psychic motivations may reinforce realistic contentions.

Simmel posits the existence of an "impulse of hostility," but makes the significant qualification that in itself this impulse does not account for conflict. In line with his general orientation, he stresses interaction as the locus of sociological and social-psychological analysis. A "primary hostility of men towards one another"[44] cannot in itself account for social conflict. Instead of relying on instincts, drives or prepotent dispositions for the explanation of social phenomena, he makes it clear that behavior always takes place in a social field and that conflict as a social phenomenon can be understood only as occurring within a pattern of interaction.

Sociologists are generally agreed that when dealing with social data, attention must be centered on the *inter*action of individuals rather than on "drives," "impulses" or other imputed properties of single individuals. It is worthy of note that modern research in psychoanalysis has amply demonstrated that human drives develop through the response which the infant receives to its social demands.[45] Even "*auto*erotic activities are absent when object relations are absent."[46] The study of children in extreme isolation shows that they can develop neither love nor hatred if they are deprived of the relationship with a love object.[47]

In view of frequent attempts to "explain" all conflict in terms of aggressive drives or needs for tension release, it seems appropriate to comment briefly upon some current developments of psychoanalytic theory on aggression.

Most contemporary psychoanalytic research proceeds on the basis of a theory of interaction. It suffices to compare earlier psychoanalytic literature on war and aggression[48] with the works of such men as Otto Fenichel, Erich Fromm, Abram Kardiner, Heinz Hartmann, Harry Stack Sullivan, to become aware of the shift that has taken place in psychoanalytic thinking. These recent analysts have accepted the concept that Malinowski in an apt phrase has called "the harnessing of aggression by culture."[49] Far from explaining social conflict merely in terms of the inherent attributes of human beings *qua* human beings, they feel that the variables of social position and cultural norms will help to account for the social phenomenon of aggression and war. Merton[50] has shown in great detail that the behavioral sciences often have failed to treat these three variables systematically and that a fourth variable, that of the social structure, has been particularly neglected.

Experimental social psychology has provided us with some significant tests of the hypothesis that the incidence of aggressive behavior is related to the structure of interactive relations. Thus, in a study of aggression by John P. French, the author deliberately introduces a structural variable: degree of group cohesion. He compares reaction to frustration among members of organized groups (basketball and football teams at Harvard) with such reaction in unorganized groups (students from introductory psychology classes at Harvard). Furthermore, he introduces a cultural variable by including in the experimental design an organized group with a different ethnic and socioeconomic background (clubs from neighborhood houses in an Italian district of East Boston).

This study showed that open in-group aggression varied positively with the degree of organization of the group.[51] "There was no direct aggression in the unorganized groups ["direct aggression" here refers to aggression expressed toward members of the group], but there were 61 instances of direct aggression in the organized group."[52] Moreover, the highest degree of aggression occurred in the organized group that came from the Italian ethnic strata—a finding which points to the influence of cultural norms on the expression of aggressiveness.[53]

The view that aggressive behavior is shaped by interaction seems to contradict our earlier distinction between realistic and nonrealistic conflict where it was suggested that nonrealistic conflict, far from arising only in the relation between an individual and the object of hatred, was to be understood as being occasioned by a release of tension against *any* suitable object. Yet the contradiction is only apparent. Aggression in nonrealistic conflict does not have to be accounted for by an urge stemming from an instinctual drive. It may be thought of as having accumulated in the interaction between the subject and others—parents or other frustrating agents—during the socialization process and in the individual's effort to live up to later role obligations. In nonrealistic conflict, the aggressive energies have accumulated in the interaction between the subject and other persons prior to the release of tension.

It becomes evident that, as Simmel says, psychic motivations are insufficient to account for conflict behavior. Realistic conflict between individuals or groups over claims for status, power, wealth or allegiance to competing systems of values *may* in their pursuit mobilize affective energies, a complex interplay of sentiments and emotions, but this is not a necessary corollary of realistic contention. Aggressiveness may be defined as a set of predispositions toward acts of aggression. Conflict, on the other hand, always denotes an interaction between two or more persons. To be sure, aggression may be regarded as in index of conflict, but this does not imply that every conflict must be accompanied by aggressiveness.

During the last war, "hatred of the enemy [i.e., aggressiveness], personal and impersonal, was not a major element in combat motivation."[54] Combat motivation was a compound of many elements, of which primary loyalties to the group of "buddies" was apparently the most important, and of which hatred of the enemy played only a minor part.[55]

Similarly, there are conflicts of interest, as for example between labor and management, in which the antagonists seem not to harbor personal feelings of hatred against each other. One frequently witnesses labor and management leaders associating closely in social life, apparently without hostile feelings against each other, while engaged in conflict in their roles as representatives of their respective groups.

Yet, as Simmel suggests, it may still be the case that "it is useful to hate the opponent." At least, this view has been behind much of the morale-building aims of propaganda, ancient or modern. If affective energy can be added to the purely realistic motivation for struggle, it is likely to strengthen the parties to the conflict. This is one reason for the superiority of citizen-soldier armies over armies composed of mercenaries.

This leads us to expect that there is a greater likelihood of admixture of nonrealistic conflict elements in groups in which the members participate with their total personality than in groups in which they participate only segmentally. This hypothesis will be discussed in Chapter IV.

[58]

HM
136
C 74

6187

CAMROSE LUTHERAN COLLEGE
LIBRARY

The distinction between objective and realistic reasons for engaging in conflict on the one hand, and the emotional energies which may be mobilized during the conflict on the other, throws some light on the function of the mediator in conflict. As Simmel has remarked, "the mediator can achieve reconcilation . . . only if each party believes that the objective situation justifies reconciliation and makes peace advantageous." The mediator shows "each party the claims and arguments of the other; they thus lose the tone of subjective passion."[56] He helps to strip the conflict of its nonrational and aggressive overtones. Yet this will not in itself allow the parties to abandon their conflicting behavior since, even boiled down to the "facts of the case," the conflicting claims remain to be dealt with. The mediator's function is primarily to eliminate tension which merely seeks release so that realistic contentions can be dealt with without interference. In addition he may suggest various ways to conduct the conflict, pointing out the relative advantages and costs of each.

Failure to realize that conflict may be motivated by two distinct yet intermingled factors—a realistic conflict situation and the affective investment in it—accounts for the weakness of certain assumptions underlying "action research" as this term is understood by the Lewin school.[57] "Action research" may indeed be most helpful in the task of differentiating the sources of realistic conflict from the emotional energies vested in it, but it can only hope to clear the road for better insights into the grounds for contention.

Simmel's proposition may now be reformulated:

Aggressive or hostile "impulses" do not suffice to account for social conflict. Hatred, just as love, needs some object. Conflict can occur only in the interaction between subject and object; it always presupposes a relationship.

Realistic conflict need not be accompanied by hostility and aggressiveness. "Tensions" in the psychological sense are not always associated with conflict behavior. Yet it might be "useful" to hate the opponent. The propagandist expects that such hatred will reinforce the emotional investment in the conflict and hence strengthen the readiness to carry it out to the end.

Conversely, the main function of the mediator is seen as divesting conflict situations of nonrealistic elements of aggressiveness so as to allow the contenders to deal realistically with the divergent claims at issue.

We have seen that the realistic conflict does not necessarily involve hostility and aggressiveness. We will have to examine next an apparently contradictory statement by Simmel, according to which hostility is an intrinsic part of social relations.*

PROPOSITION 5:

Hostility in Close Social Relationships

"While antagonism by itself does not produce sociation, it is a sociological element almost never absent in it. . . . This probably is often the situation in respect to the so-called mixture of converging and diverging currents within a group. That is, the structure may be *sui generis* . . . and only in order to be able to describe and understand it, do we put it together, *post factum*, out of two tendencies, one monistic, the other antagonistic. Erotic relations offer the most frequent illustrations. How often do they not strike us as woven together of love and respect, or disrespect . . . of love and an urge to dominate or the need for dependence. But what the observer or the participant himself divides into two intermingling trends may in reality be only one."[58]

In this proposition Simmel asserts that social relationships are likely to involve both converging and diverging motivations, both "love and hatred," which generally are intricately linked. One frequently hates the person one loves; hence it is often invalid to separate the two elements in concrete reality. It is a

---

* Henceforth, the term "conflict" will apply to realistic conflict only.

misconception to think of the one factor building up what the other factor has torn down.

One clarification needs to be introduced immediately if this statement is not to contradict the earlier propositions. If hatred were indeed a part of every relationship, there could not be any realistic conflict situations in which such feelings have no part. However, it appears, although he does not make this sufficiently clear, that Simmel actually refers to close and intimate relationships rather than to all social relationships; his reference to erotic relationships as his key example seems to indicate this.

Simmel implies that in relationships in which the participants are deeply involved, in which they are engaged with their total personality rather than with only a segment of it, there will probably arise feelings of both love and hatred, both attraction and hostility.

This is reminiscent of the Freudian concept of *ambivalence*,[59] which has now become a central concept in psychoanalysis. Ambivalence is defined by Freud as "a directing of antithetical feelings (affectionate and hostile) toward the same person,"[60] essentially the situation Simmel has in mind. Freud, however, actually describes the psychological source of the phenomenon which Simmel simply observes. This psychoanalytic concept will therefore help to clarify and supplement Simmel's proposition.

Freud develops his analysis of ambivalence in social relations in *Group Psychology and the Analysis of the Ego*,[61] where he writes:

> Almost every intimate emotional relation between two people which lasts for some time—marriage, friendship, the relations between parents and children—leaves a sediment of feelings of aversion and hostility, which have first to be eliminated by repression. This is less disguised in the common wrangles between business partners or in the grumbles of a subordinate at his superior. The same thing happens when men come together in large units. Every time two families become connected by marriage, each of them thinks itself superior to or of better birth than the other. Of two neighboring towns, each is the other's most jealous rival. . . . When this hostility is directed against

people who are otherwise loved, we describe it as ambivalence of feeling; and we explain the fact, in what is probably far too rational a manner, by means of the numerous occasions for conflicts of interest which arise precisely in such intimate relations.

We note that, like Simmel, Freud derives ambivalence of feelings from the intimacy of the relationship within which it occurs. He traces the simultaneity of feelings of love and hate to the numerous occasions for conflict to which intimate relations give rise.

This would mean that there is more occasion for the rise of hostile feelings in primary than in secondary groups, for the more the relationship is based upon the participation of the total personality—as distinct from segmental participation—the more it is likely to generate both love and hate.[62]

The closer the relationship, the greater the affective investment, the greater also the tendency to suppress rather than express hostile feelings. Whereas in secondary relationships, such as with business partners, feelings of hostility can be expressed with relative freedom, this is not always the case in primary relationships where total involvement of the participants may make the acting out of such feelings a danger to the relationship. In such cases feelings of hostility tend to accumulate and hence to intensify.

"Intimacy" or "closeness" remains an as yet unanalyzed term. Following Homans' theory[63] that there is a correlation between the increase of interaction of the participants in a relationship and the increase of their mutual sentiments of liking, we may say that the intense interaction which is characteristic of primary groups and of relations approaching the primary group type tends to involve the total personality and hence to strengthen intimacy of feelings. But Homans overlooked the fact that it is precisely this intimacy which also generates accumulation of hostile feelings, since it furnishes frequent occasions for conflict which may often be suppressed for the sake of the affectionate sentiments.[64] Homans' lack of concern with the ambivalent character of intimate social relations unfortunately prevents him from observing that an increase in social interaction is likely to bring about an increase of hostility as well as of liking.[65]

In addition to psychoanalysis and sociology, anthropology also has made contributions toward the clarification of this problem. Bronislaw Malinowski writes:[66] "Aggression like charity begins at home. [The examples given] all imply direct contact and then the flaring up of anger over immediate issues, where divergent interests occur, or . . . are imagined to occur. Indeed the smaller the group engaged in co-operation, united by some common interests, and living day by day with one another, the easier it is for them to be mutually irritated and to flare up in anger."[67] "Aggression is a by-product of co-operation. . . . Let us try to understand the place of aggressiveness within an institution. There is no doubt at all, within these shortrange co-operative and spatially condensed forms of human organization, genuine aggressiveness will occur more readily and universally than anywhere else."[68]

Malinowski agrees with Simmel and Freud that antagonism is a central part of intimate social relations, that it is a "by-product" of co-operation. But while Simmel, Freud and Homans refer to *feelings*, Malinowski states that hostile *behavior* also occurs more readily in close social relations. The next proposition will discuss this related yet separate problem.

It still remains to be indicated that in certain cases there exist institutional channels for the manifestation of ambivalence. The so-called "joking relationship" between clans and between relatives by marriage which has been described by anthropologists embodies such a merging of elements of friendliness and mutual aid with hostility. Radcliffe-Brown[69] describes the structural situation, in joking relationships between two clans as follows:

The individual is a member of a certain defined group . . . within which his relations to others are defined by a complex set of rights and duties. . . . But beyond the field within which social relations are thus defined, there lie other groups with which . . . the relation involves possible or actual hostility In

[63]

any fixed relations between the members of two such groups the separateness of the groups must be recognized. It is precisely this separateness which is emphasized when a joking relationship is established. The show of hostility, the perpetual disrespect, is a continual expression of that social disjunction which is an essential part of the whole structural situation, but over which, without destroying or even weakening it, there is provided the social conjunction of friendliness and mutual aid. . . . The joking relationship which constitutes an alliance between clans or tribes, and that between relatives by marriage, are modes of organizing a definite and stable system of social behavior in which conjunctive and disjunctive components . . . are maintained and combined.

In this case the combination of both elements makes the relation possible and allows it to exist. The joking relationship can serve binding functions only if it allows at the same time mutual expression of hostility.[70]

As distinct from the cases discussed earlier, ambivalence here does not arise as a consequence of closeness of relationships, but closer relationships can be achieved only if special institutional means are provided for the concomitant expression of hostility and attraction. In other words, the bond between the participating persons or groups is not initially close, and yet a closer relationship is judged desirable by them. In such cases, institutional channels for expression of "love *cum* hatred" feelings facilitate the establishment of the relationship, just as the safety-valve institution facilitates its maintenance.

Reformulating the present proposition, we may say that antagonism is usually involved as an element in intimate relationships. Converging and diverging motivations may be so commingled in the actual relationship that they can be separated only for classificatory and analytical purposes, while the relationship actually has a unitary character *sui generis*.

Close social relationships, characterized as they are by frequent interaction and involving the total personality of the participants, may be said to include in their motivational structure an essential ambivalence in that they contain both positive and negative cathexes inextricably intertwined.

We will move on to consider the corollary of this proposition: that intensity of conflict is related to closeness of the relationship.

CHAPTER IV

IN-GROUP CONFLICT
AND GROUP STRUCTURE

PROPOSITION 6:

The Closer the Relationship,
the More Intense the Conflict

"A hostility must excite consciousness the more deeply and violently, the greater the parties' similarity against the background of which the hostility arises. . . . People who have many common features often do one another worse or 'worser' wrong than complete strangers do. . . . We confront the stranger with whom we share neither characteristics nor broader interests, objectively; we hold our personalities in reserve. . . . The more we have in common with another *as whole persons*, however, the more easily will our totality be involved in every single relation to him. . . . Therefore, if a quarrel arises between persons in such an intimate relationship, it is often so passionately expansive. . . .

"The second type which is relevant here . . . is the case of a hostility whose intensification is grounded in a feeling of belonging together, of unity . . . [this shows] the peculiar phenomenon of social hatred. This hatred is directed against a member of the group, not from personal motives, but because the member presents a danger to the preservation of the group. . . . The two conflicting parties hate each other not only on the concrete ground which produced the conflict but also on the sociological ground of hatred for the enemy of the group itself. . . . Typical of this is the way the renegade hates and is hated. The recall of earlier agreement has such a strong effect that the new contrast is infinitely sharper and bitterer than if no relation at all had existed in the past . . . 'respect for the enemy' is usually absent where the hostility has arisen on the basis of previous solidarity. And where enough similarities continue to make confusions and blurred borderlines possible, points of difference need an emphasis not justified by the issue but only by that danger of confusion."[1]

SIMMEL'S STATEMENT that close ties and great involvement make for much more intense conflict, when conflict occurs at all, is a corollary of the results described in the preceding discussion. The ambivalence generally present in close relationships was said to stem from the suppression of hostile feelings (which in turn were traced to the frequent occasions for conflict inherent in such relationships), the acting out of which is being avoided by the participants for fear of the disruptive effects of such conflicts. If the "love object" is at the same time a "hate object," it is understandable that conflict would mobilize the entire affect of the personality and that the relationship might be disrupted through the resultant intense conflict; hence there is a tendency to suppression.

It will be remembered that an earlier discussion of the reinforcing effect of nonrealistic elements in realistic conflict situations led to the hypothesis that the intensity of conflict will be likely to increase through such admixture. Thus a greater intensity of conflict can be expected in those relationships in which the participants have been led to suppress hostile feelings. So the fear of intense conflict may lead to suppression of hostile feelings; and in turn, the accumulation of such feelings is likely to further intensify the conflict once it breaks out.

In groups that appeal only to a peripheral part of their members' personality, or, to use Parsons' terminology,[2] in groups in which relations are functionally specific and affectively neutral, conflicts are apt to be less sharp and violent than in groups wherein ties are diffuse and affective, engaging the total personality of their members. In effect, this suggests that conflicts in groups such as Rotary Clubs or Chambers of Commerce are likely to be less violent than in groups such as religious sects or radical parties of the Communist type. Organizations of the latter kind aim at encompassing the total personality, hence the bond between the members is much stronger there than in groups where segmental types of relations prevail. If total personalities are involved, there is also a greater likelihood that nonrealistic elements will enter into realistic conflict situations. Hence such groups will tend to suppress conflict, but if it occurs nevertheless, it will be intense and passionate. This, as will be seen later, accounts for the frequency of splits and disruptions in such groups.

Individuals who participate intensely in the life of such groups are concerned with the group's continuance. If they witness the breaking away of one with whom they have shared cares and responsibilities of group life, they are likely to react in a more violent way against such "disloyalty" than less involved members. This leads to Simmel's second point: renegadism is perceived by a close group as a threat to its unity.

We shall consider later how groups, when threatened by other groups, may be forced to "pull themselves together." Here we note that a similar reaction occurs in the defense of the close group against a danger from within. Indeed, as Simmel suggests, the reaction may be stronger under these conditions because the "enemy" from within, the renegade or heretic, not only puts into question the values and interests of the group, but also threatens its very unity. Renegadism signifies and symbolizes a desertion of those standards of the group considered vital to its well-being, if not to its actual existence.[3]

We maintained earlier that conflict with an out-group defines the boundaries of the in-group. Conversely, renegadism threatens to break down the boundary lines of the established group. Therefore the group must fight the renegade with all its might since he threatens symbolically, if not in fact, its existence as an ongoing concern. In the religious sphere, for example, apostasy strikes at the very life of a church, hence the violence of denunciation of the apostate contained in the pronouncements of early Church fathers or in rabbinical statements from the time of the Maccabees onward.[4]

The renegade contributes to the strength of the out-group to which he transfers his allegiance not only, as Simmel points out,[5] because, unable to go back, he will be more firm in his loyalty to the new group than those who have belonged to it all along, but also because he gives it the increased conviction of the righteousness of its cause. This in itself makes him more dangerous in the eyes of his former associates than any other member of the out-group. Furthermore, not only will the renegade emphasize his loyalty to the new group by engaging in its defense and crusading for its values, but, as Max Scheler has pointed out, he will also see it as his chief goal to "engage in a continuous chain of acts of revenge on his spiritual past."[6] Thus his attack on the values of his previous group does not cease with his departure, but continues long after the rupture has been completed. To the group he has left, he appears as a symbol of the danger in which the group finds itself in the face of potential enemy attack.

The heretic presents a somewhat different problem to the group than does the apostate. At times the reaction of the group against the heretic is even more hostile than against the apostate. Whereas the latter deserts the group in order to go over to the enemy, the heretic presents a more insidious danger: by upholding the group's central values and goals, he threatens to split it into factions that will differ as to the means for implementing its goal. Unlike the apostate, the heretic claims to uphold the group's values and interests, only proposing different means to this end or variant interpretations of the official creed. Heresy derives from a Greek verb which means "to choose" or "to take for oneself." The heretic proposes alternatives where the group wants no alternative to exist.[7] As Robert Michels wrote, "The hatred of the party is directed, not in the first place against the opponents of its own view of the world order, but against the dreaded rivals in the political field, *against those who are competing for the same end*."[8] In this respect, the heretic calls forth all the more hostility in that he still has much in common with his former fellow-members in sharing their goals.

It is less dangerous for a group if the one who breaks with it goes over to the enemy than if, as a heretic, he forms his own rival group (hence the attempt to brand as "agents of the enemy" former group members who have left in dissension). The heretic continues to compete for the loyalty of the members of his former group even after he has left it. The renegade will fight them, the heretic will proselytize. Moreover, by professing to share the values of the group, the heretic creates confusion and hence his actions are perceived as an attempt to break down the boundaries. This is one of the reasons why Trotsky appeared to Stalin as a more serious danger than General Vlassov, and why Lenin's most violent denunciatory language is not directed against any capitalist but is reserved for Karl Kautsky.

However, a weakening of the group is not a necessary result of such struggles. On the contrary, the perception of this inside "danger" on the part of the remaining group members makes for their "pulling together," for an increase in their awareness of the issues at stake, and for an increase in participation; in short, the danger signal brings about the mobilization of all group defenses.[9] Just because the struggle concentrates the group's energies for purposes of self-defense, it ties the members more closely to each other and promotes group integration. The Catholic Church owed much of its doctrinal and organizational vigor to its struggles against Gnostic and Manichaean heresies and its later conflicts with Protestant reformers.

Paraphrasing Simmel's proposition, we may say that a conflict is more passionate and more radical when it arises out of close relationships. The coexistence of union and opposition in such relations makes for the peculiar sharpness of the conflict. Enmity calls forth deeper and more violent reactions, the greater the involvement of the parties among whom it originates.

In conflicts within a close group, one side hates the other more intensely the more it is felt to be a threat to the unity and the identity of the group.[10]

Greater participation in the group and greater personality involvement of the members provide greater opportunity to engage in intense conflicting behavior and hence more violent reactions against disloyalty. It is in this sense that intense conflict and group loyalty are two facets of the same relation.

In the last proposition we stated that hostile feelings are likely to arise in close relationships and that if conflicts occur in these relationships, they are likely to be intense. This does not necessarily point to the likelihood of more *frequent* conflict in closer relationships than in less close ones. We have already encountered situations in which accumulated hostility does not eventuate in conflict behavior. The next proposition will consider this problem further.

PROPOSITION 7:

Impact and Function of Conflict
in Group Structures

"Contradiction and conflict not only precede unity but are operative in it at every moment of its existence. . . . There probably exists no social unit in which convergent and divergent currents among its members are not inseparably interwoven. . . .

"Conflict is designed to resolve divergent dualisms; it is a way of achieving some kind of unity. . . . This is roughly parallel to the fact that it is the most violent symptom of a disease which represent the effort of the organism to free itself of disturbances and damages caused by them. . . . Conflict itself resolves the tension between contrasts."[11]

In the two previous propositions we examined some of the relations between hostile feelings, conflict and the structure of the relationship within which they occur. We have contended that the closer the relationship and the more the participants are involved in it, the more occasions there are for conflict. The more frequent the interaction, the more occasion for hostile interaction.

Yet, frequent *occasions* for conflict do not necessarily eventuate in frequent conflicts. It is precisely the closeness of the relationship and the strong affective mutual attachment of the participants which may induce them to avoid the conflict. Such suppression may lead to further intensification of the conflict once it breaks out.

Closeness and consequently a relatively high degree of involvement of the personality make it likely that conflict will assume greater intensity. Discussing the situation of the Jews after their emancipation, Kurt Lewin, in full agreement with Simmel, implies that, as the Jewish group becomes more integrated into the general community, conflict increases in intensity as a result of the increase in interaction.[12]

The relation between group structure and conflict can now be further pursued. It is Simmel's contention in the above proposition, as in the bulk of his essay, that conflict is a component of all social relationships and that it fulfills positive functions inasmuch as it leads to the re-establishment of unity and balance in the group.

But does conflict always re-establish unity, or does this happen only under a specific set of circumstances? We are led to ask: if conflict unites, what tears apart? This raises a related question: can we assume that *conflicts over different types of issues* are likely to have the same impact on a given relationship, and that *every type of structure* is equally benefited by conflict?

It would appear that Simmel has failed to make a distinction between conflicts which concern the very basis of a relationship and those which concern less central issues. Conflicts arising within the same consensual framework are likely to have a very different impact upon the relationship than those which put the basic consensus in question. Thus, within a marriage relation, a conflict on whether or not to have children involves the basic consensual agreement about the very purposes of the relationship. One may expect that this type of conflict will presumably have a more profound impact on the relationship than a conflict over particular plans to spend a vacation or to allocate the family budget.

Such a distinction, between conflicts over basic matters of principle and conflicts over matters presupposing adherence to the same basic principle, has long been made in political theory, although it has been comparatively neglected in the study of other spheres of human interaction. Thus Ortega y Gasset, the Spanish philosopher, commenting on Cicero's *De Republica*, writes:

> Far from extolling peace or regarding public life as a matter of suave urbanity, Cicero held *dissensiones civiles* to be the very condition on which the welfare of the state is based and from which it derives. . . . Intestine strife, Cicero had read in Aristotle, arises when members of a society disagree about political matters —a somewhat hackneyed statement. However, have we not just seen that discord may also give the impulse for further development and perfection of the state? On the other hand, a society obviously relies for its existence upon common consent in certain ultimate matters. Such unanimity Cicero called *concordia*, and he defines it as "the best bond of permanent union in any commonwealth." How does the one tally with the other? Quite easily, if we picture the body of opinion from which the life of a nation draws its sustenance as made up of various layers. Divergencies in surface layers produce beneficient conflict because the ensuing struggles move upon the firm ground of deeper concord. Questioning certain things, but not questioning all, minor divergencies serve but to confirm and consolidate the underlying unanimity of the collective existence. But if dissent affects the basic layers of common belief on which the solidarity of the social body lastly rests, then the state becomes a house divided, society dis-sociates, splitting up into two societies—that is two groups with fundamentally divergent beliefs.[13]

A similar view informs modern political thought. John Stuart Mill states that it is possible to pass through turbulent times without permanent weakening of the political structure only if: "However important the interest about which men fall out, the conflict did not affect the fundamental principles of the system of social union."[14]

The distinction between conflicts over the basis of consensus and those taking place within the basic consensus, comprises part of the common ground of political science from Aristotle to modern political theory. Though, as has been said, other social sciences have not been as clearly aware of this distinction, several sociologists have recognized it. George Simpson, in one of the few contemporary discussions of the positive and integrative functions of conflict, distinguishes between what, following Robert MacIver, he calls communal and non-communal conflicts: "Non-communal conflict results when there is no community of ends between the parties to the conflict, or when these parties believe that no common ends can be discovered so that a compromise may be reached." "Non-communal conflict is seen as disruptive and dissociating. Communal conflict, i.e., that based on a common acceptance of basic ends, is, on the contrary, integrative." "When men settle their differences on the basis of unity, communal conflict will ensue; when they settle their unity upon these differences, non-communal conflict will ensue."[15]

Yet the distinction which Ortega y Gasset, Mill and Simpson make would serve us little unless we should be able to indicate under what conditions conflicts are likely to assume the extreme character of which they speak.

The very interdependence of groups and individuals in modern society checks to some extent tendencies toward basic cleavages. What Durkheim said of the individual in the society of organic solidarity applies equally to groups: just as the individual "depends upon society because he depends upon the parts of which it is composed,"[16] groups also, due to their interdependence, help to maintain the social system within which they function. In general, the division of labor creates interdependence and hence exerts pressure against radical breaks away from the system.

As Wilbert Moore has pointed out,[17] most American unions recognize their dependence upon the continued survival of the business. A similar recognition of dependence, he says, underlies all conflict relations—e.g., church and state, family and school—where there are separate and interdependent functions.

[75]

Yet interdependence, while checking tendencies toward a radical break with the system, is no bar to differences of interest leading to conflict; on the contrary, the greater the interdependence, the sharper the focus of attention upon questions of relative advantage. As E. T. Hiller has said: "Co-operation produces dependence, and withholding co-operation provides each party with a means of coercion and of opposition against the other."[18]

Thus interdependence is at the same time a check against the breaking of consensual agreement and a basis for that conflicting behavior which is not likely to have disruptive consequences.

Interdependence checks basic cleavages. It does not follow from this that closeness brings about similar checks, for functional interdependence is not associated with closeness of relationships. It would seem that the contrary is the case. If relationships are close, it was noted, there is a tendency for conflict, whenever it breaks out, to be particularly intense. We may now add that such intense conflicts are more likely to touch upon the basic consensual agreement. Indeed, this seems often to be the case in the close group. May we not expect, then, that loosely organized groups, those in which members participate segmentally rather than with their total personality, are less likely to experience intensified conflict leading to disruption? Given segmental participation, the very multiplicity of conflicts in itself tends to constitute a check against the breakdown of consensus. It has been suggested by Edward Alsworth Ross, for example, that:

Every species of social conflict interferes with every other species in society . . . save only when lines of cleavage coincide; in which case they reinforce one another. . . . These different oppositions in society are like different wave series set upon opposite sides of a lake, which neutralize each other if the crest of one meets the trough of the other, but which reinforce each other if crest meets crest while trough meets trough. . . . A society, therefore, which is ridden by a dozen oppositions along lines running in every direction may actually be in less danger of being torn with violence or falling to pieces than one split just along one line. For each new cleavage contributes to narrow the cross clefts, so that one might say that *society is sewn to-gether* by its inner conflicts.[19]

This idea merits further discussion, for it seems to contain an insight which extends Simmel's contention that conflict has positive functions. Stability within a loosely structured society, often inadequately identified with the absence of conflict, can be viewed as partly a product of the continuous incidence of various conflicts crisscrossing it. The stability, for instance, of bureaucratic structures, may be accounted for in part by the fact that a multiplicity of conflicts (between various bureaus and offices, as well as between various office-holders along many divergent lines) prevents the formation of a united front (for example, low-status against high-status members of the hierarchy). If, on the other hand, *one* conflict cuts through a group, dividing the members into two hostile camps—and this seems more likely to occur in close groups—the single cleavage will very probably put into question the basic consensual agreement, thus endangering the continued existence of the group.[20]

It may be that one reason for the relative absence of "class struggle" in this country is the fact that the American worker, far from restricting his allegiance to class-conflict groupings and associations, is a member of a number of associations and groupings which represent him in diverse conflicts with different religious, ethnic, status and political groups. Since the lines of conflict between all these groups do not converge, the cleavage along class lines does not draw the total energies and allegiance of the worker into a single area of conflict. The relative stability of the American class structure (as compared with European class structures) and the failure of Marxian—or Syndicalist Sorelian—attempts to divorce the American worker from non-class types of allegiances seem to confirm this observation.

Similarly, many a professional society seems to owe its structural stability partly to the fact that, although it may include a number of sharply differing views, these "cancel out" because they do not cumulate around one central issue. If American geneticists were to divide between the followers of Mendel and

Weismann on the one hand and those of Lysenko on the other, it would not augur well for the stability of their professional organization!

One of the traditional Protestant arguments against Catholics in this country, as well as one of the traditional arguments against Communists, is precisely that these organizations attempt to capture the total allegiance of their members, thus insulating them against the customary cross-conflicts of American society.[21]

Ross's main idea may now be further clarified. It is implied that individuals affiliate with a multiplicity of groups in a society where, Ross asserts, the crisscrossing of conflict has stabilizing functions. But multiple affiliations alone would not produce the consequences which Ross points out. If the members of a society should have mutually reinforcing interests, multiple affiliations, instead of crisscrossing each other, would eventually consolidate into basic cleavages. Only if there are numerous antagonistic yet diversified interests will the likelihood of consolidation in a cluster of affiliations be avoided and segmentation of participation maintained.

This suggests a problem which has been almost completely neglected in current sociological theory. Multiple group affiliations and conflicting roles have been considered primarily, if not almost exclusively, as a source of psychic conflicts for the individuals who are said to be torn between incompatible loyalties and allegiances. Such inner conflicts as those arising from membership in the church and in the business community, from membership in primary groups and in bureaucratic organizations, have been examined in great detail. However, it is not chiefly with the emergence of inner tensions among individual affiliates that sociological (as distinct from social-psychological) analysis should concern itself, but primarily with the significance of group and role conflicts for the structure as a whole. This pattern of multiple group affiliations with conflicting interests and values can be profitably examined in terms of its functional significance for the structure of the society. If we follow the clues provided by Simmel and Ross, we come to see that the multiple group affiliations of individuals make for a multiplicity of conflicts criss-crossing society. Such segmental participation, then, can result in a kind of balancing mechanism, preventing deep cleavages along one axis. The interdependence of conflicting groups and the multiplicity of noncumulative conflicts provide one, though not, of course, the only check against basic consensual break-down in an open society.

Rigid systems, such as contemporary totalitarian societies, may succeed, as has been suggested previously, in partly canalizing hostile feelings through safety-valve institutions such as institutionalized anti-Semitism or xenophobia. However, their lack of mechanisms for readjustment to changed conditions permits the accumulation of occasions for conflict and hence of hostilities which may eventually directly threaten consensual agreement.

Flexible systems, on the contrary, by allowing occurrences of conflict, make the danger of breakdowns of consensual agreements remote. If this is the case, the expression and acting out of hostile feelings through conflict leads to mutual and unilateral accommodation and adjustments between component parts.

Institutionalized channels for carrying out such conflicts would seem to constitute an important "balancing mechanism" in a society. Shifting relations of strength which are revealed in and through conflicts between various groups can be dealt with through continuous readjustments so that the basic structure remains flexible enough to withstand internal strains. Consequently, in such flexible systems the danger of conflicts disturbing the basic consensus is minimized.

Our conclusions regarding the functions of conflict in societies and in less complex relationships are thus essentially similar. Close relationships, though providing frequent occasions for conflicts, exhibit tendencies toward the suppression of these conflicts. If, however, conflicts occur despite suppression, they tend to disrupt the relationship because they are likely to assume peculiar intensity due to the total involvement of the personality and the accumulation of suppressed hostilities. Similarly, societies that claim total individual involvement of their members fear and suppress conflict, but are threatened by the danger of disruptive outbreaks. Pluralistic societies, however, which are built on multiple group affiliation tend to be "sewn together" by multiple and multiform conflicts between groups in which the members' personalities are involved only segmentally.

We can now say that feelings of enmity need not always be diverted or result in ambivalence if the group or society is to be maintained. Far from upsetting the basic relationship, the direct expression of feelings of enmity can be a source of integration if participation is segmental rather than total. Ambivalence or displacement would occur much more frequently where the relationship is close and where the participants fear that any attack would immediately threaten its very foundation. Discontent that expresses itself wherever and whenever it occurs, that is not left to accumulate and to become channeled into one major cleavage, helps to maintain the society or group.

Simmel's proposition may now be reformulated as follows: Conflict may serve to remove dissociating elements in a relationship and to re-establish unity. Insofar as conflict is the resolution of tension between antagonists it has stabilizing functions and becomes an integrating component of the relationship. However, not all conflicts are positively functional for the relationship, but only those which concern goals, values or interests that do not contradict the basic assumptions upon which the relation is founded. Loosely structured groups and open societies, by allowing conflicts, institute safeguards against the type of conflict which would endanger basic consensus and thereby minimize the danger of divergences touching core values. The interdependence of antagonistic groups and the crisscrossing within such societies of conflicts, which serve to "sew the social system together" by cancelling each other out, thus prevent disintegration along one primary line of cleavage.

The following proposition will once more concern the relation between conflict and group structure, but will introduce an additional factor, namely, the stability of a relationship.

PROPOSITION 8:

Conflict as an Index of Stability of Relationships

"It is by no means the sign of the most genuine and deep affection never to yield to occasions for conflict. . . . On the contrary, this behavior often characterizes attitudes which lack the ultimate unconditional devotion. . . . The felt insecurity concerning the basis of such relations often moves us, who desire to maintain the relations at all costs, to acts of exaggerated selflessness, to the almost mechanical insurance of the relationship through the avoidance on principle, of every possible conflict. Where on the other hand we are certain of the irrevocability and unreservedness of our feeling, such peace at any price is not necessary. We know that no crisis can penetrate to the foundation of the relationship."[22]

IT IS SIMMEL'S CONTENTION in this proposition that the absence of conflict within a relationship cannot serve as an index of its underlying stability. We note that he does not assert that the presence of conflict necessarily indicates basic stability but only that, given the presence of hostile feelings in a relationship, these feelings are more likely to be expressed in conflict if this relationship is stable.

Simmel thus suggests that hostile feelings generated within a relationship are more likely to be expressed if the participants are aware of its stability, for if they are secure they will tend to express their feelings freely. However, if the relationship is such that the participants must fear its dissolution if conflict occurs, they will attempt to repress or displace hostile feelings.

The most general supposition in Simmel's statement touches upon a central point in sociological method. Simmel contends that it is necessary for one to probe beneath behavioral manifestations in order to disclose the full extent of social reality.

Thus, according to Simmel, the lack of conflict in a relationship cannot be taken to indicate that the relationship is stable and secure or that it is free from potentially disruptive strains. We must concern ourselves with latent as well as with manifest elements within a relationship if its full meaning is to be disclosed analytically.[23]

So, if we are concerned with ascertaining whether a relationship is stable, Simmel suggests that it will not suffice to inquire whether elements of conflict are apparent since the absence of conflict behavior alone cannot serve as an index of the absence of strain and hostile sentiments.

To take a concrete illustration: it would be imprudent to conclude from the absence of conflict in race relations that there is interracial adjustment. The lack of conflict between Negroes and whites in the South, in contrast to frequent conflicts in race relations in many a Northern city, has often been taken to indicate that Negro-white relations are more stable in the South. Such a conclusion appears to be unjustified. The absence of conflict in itself does not indicate the absence of feelings of hostility and antagonism and hence absence of elements of strain and malintegration.

Yet, Simmel does not stop at this distinction between social appearance and social reality. He provides us with a useful clue for deducing underlying conditions from behavior. Contrary to what common sense might seem to indicate, Simmel asserts that in close relationships where, as we have seen, hostile feelings are likely to be present, the very absence of conflict might be taken as an index of the existence of underlying elements of strain. He asserts that if the participants in a close relationship view this relationship as tenuous, if they feel that the bonds between them cannot withstand the expression of their sentiments of hostility and if they fear the severance of the relationship, they will attempt to avoid acting out their hostile feelings.

Earlier propositions have pointed to the fact that in close relationships many occasions for conflict are likely to arise. We then concluded that the reason for the relative infrequency of actual conflicts in such relationships seems to be due to the fact that the participants, fearing the intensity of conflict as a result of their close involvement, tend to suppress its occurrence.

We can now introduce the likelihood of occurrence of conflicts in such relationships as an index of their stability. If the relationship is stable, if, in other words, the participants feel that it will not be endangered by conflict, conflicts are likely to arise between them.

The peculiar intensity of conflicts in close relationships was said to result from the accumulation of hostility. We may now add that if in close relationships each occasion for conflict leads to immediate acting out rather than to suppression of hostility, no cumulation of hostility will occur and the relationship will exhibit neither the ambivalence of feelings of which we spoke earlier in Proposition 5, nor the intensity which was discussed in Proposition 6.

Simmel's idea may be illustrated by a reference to current research in family relations. Contemporary marriage prediction analysis relies heavily upon the incidence of conflict (as reported by the married pair or by outside observers) as a criterion for predicting success or failure in marriage.[24] It is generally concluded in studies of this type that a marriage beset by many conflicts is less likely to endure than one where no conflicts are reported. Following the lead provided by Simmel, we must raise two main queries concerning these studies: (1) Can we assume that the absence of conflict behavior is necessarily correlated with the absence of hostile feelings, and hence indicates a stable adjustment between the married pair? (2) May not the occurrence of marital conflict in certain situations, given the likelihood of the presence of hostile feelings in a close marriage relationship, indicate the strength rather than the weakness of the relationship between the partners? In other words, may we not be led to expect more stable integration of the marriage relationship if some conflicts occur? Presence of conflict might indicate that the partners are not reluctant to express hostile sentiments, that they do not fear that such behavior might harm the stability of the relationship.[25]

Turning now to secondary relationships, we note that what has been said for primary groups applies here *a fortiori*. In secondary relationships there arise occasions for conflict, but since these tend to involve only segments of the participants' personality, they tend to be less intense and not to constitute a threat of disruption of basic consensual agreements between them. Multiple-group societies were said to benefit from many conflicts criss-crossing each other. If this statement is accepted, it follows that conflict in such societies, far from constituting an index of imbalance, is an index of the operation of a balancing mechanism.

To illustrate this point, let us consider the occurrence of conflicts between racial groups. Such conflicts may, under certain conditions, be taken as an index of the better integration of a minority group in the total community. A minority group which, though linked to a majority group, feels that the uniting bond is unstable, will lack the security which is needed to act out hostility in conflict. It will tend instead to harbor toward the majority group ambivalent feelings in which positive sentiments of admiration and respect are commingled with feelings of rejection and hatred.[26] To the extent that members of the minority group do act out their conflicts with the majority group, we would expect to find that they are secure enough in their relations with that group to risk such expression and that they feel the consensual bond between them to be strong enough to withstand antagonistic action.[27]

A study of the attitudes of Negroes in the Army during the last war reveals that those Negroes who were most positively motivated toward the war, who were most ready to volunteer for combat, were precisely those who tended to be most militant concerning race relations.[28]

To cite another example, studies of voluntary associations show that not only are those members who are most deeply committed to group goals and purposes more likely to turn up at meetings, but also those same members who have a stable bond with the organization tend to be the ones who are most likely to engage in conflict with the leadership of the group.[29]

Frequent conflict in such associations, far from necessarily indicating their instability might, on the contrary, indicate that a relatively high proportion of the membership actually is involved in the life of the group.

Simmel's proposition may be reformulated as follows:

The absence of conflict cannot be taken as an index of the strength and stability of a relationship. Stable relationships may be characterized by conflicting behavior. Closeness gives rise to frequent occasions for conflict, but if the participants feel that their relationships are tenuous, they will avoid conflict, fearing that it might endanger the continuance of the relation. When close relationships are characterized by frequent conflicts rather than by the accumulation of hostile and ambivalent feelings, we may be justified, given that such conflicts are not likely to concern basic consensus, in taking these frequent conflicts as an index of the stability of these relationships.

In secondary relationships, where we are initially justified in expecting relatively less intense conflicts owing to the segmental involvement of the participants, the presence of conflict may be taken as an index of the operation of a balancing mechanism.

The next propositions will deal primarily with the functions for the in-group of conflict with other groups, but there will still be occasion to consider problems of conflict within the in-group.

CHAPTER V

CONFLICT WITH OUT-GROUPS AND GROUP STRUCTURE

PROPOSITION 9:

Conflict with Out-Groups Increases Internal Cohesion

"The group in a state of peace can permit antagonistic members within it to live with one another in an undecided situation because each of them can go his own way and can avoid collisions. A state of conflict, however, pulls the members so tightly together and subjects them to such uniform impulse that they either must get completely along with, or completely repel, one another. This is the reason why war with the outside is sometimes the last chance for a state ridden with inner antagonisms to overcome these antagonisms, or else to break up definitely.

"The fighter must 'pull himself together.' That is, all his energies must be, as it were, concentrated in one point so that they can be employed at any moment in any required direction.

"The well-known reciprocal relation between a despotic orientation and the warlike tendencies of a group rests on this informal basis: war needs a centralistic intensification of the group form, and this is guaranteed best by despotism."[1]

THIS AND THE FOLLOWING PROPOSITIONS attempt a more detailed discussion of the impact of conflict with another group upon group structure.

It was suggested earlier that group boundaries are established through conflict with the outside, so that a group defines itself by struggling with other groups. Simmel goes on to suggest that outside conflict will strengthen the internal cohesion of the group and increase centralization.

We must now raise a problem that Simmel ignored throughout his essay. He tends to move indiscriminately from conflicts which do not involve the use of violence to struggles which assume the form of warfare. Although it is legitimate to uncover similarities underlying all forms of conflict, yet, as we shall see, indiscriminate lumping of warfare with other forms of conflict will at times lead to untenable conclusions.

Since Simmel here treats warfare as illustrative of conflict, we will first consider the effect of war upon the social organization of modern nations.

The function of war in the rise of the modern centralized state has been pointed out so frequently and elaborated upon in such detail that an extended discussion of the subject seems to be superfluous. Whether in the theories of Ludwig Gumplowicz,[2] Gustav Ratzenhofer[3] and Franz Oppenheimer[4] about the central role of forcible conquest and war in the genesis of the state, or in the somewhat more guarded statements of Sumner that "war intensifies societal organization,"[5] the interdependence of centralization and war suggested by Simmel has not been questioned.

Most modern sociologists would reject Herbert Spencer's schematic distinction between the militant and the industrial type of society;[6] yet few would quarrel with his surprisingly modern statement that "the efforts of all being utilized directly or indirectly for war, will be most effectual when they are most combined; and, besides union among the combatants, there must be such union among the non-combatants with them as renders the aid of these fully and promptly available. To satisfy these requirements, the life, the actions, and the possessions of each individual must be held at the service of society.[7]

What Alexis de Tocqueville called "the first axiom of science," namely, that "war does not always give over democratic communities to military government, but it must invariably and immeasurably increase the powers of civil government; it must almost compulsorily concentrate the direction of all men and the management of all things in the hands of administration,"[8] will be found by most sociological observers to be even more applicable to our day than it was to Tocqueville's.

There exists a full convergence on this point between the views of Max Weber and those of his contemporary, Simmel. Weber maintains that "the discipline of the army gives birth to all disciplines,"[9] and bureaucracy, in its turn, is discipline's "most rational offspring."[10] Weber's whole discussion of the modern state with its centralized bureaucratic system is to a large extent predicated on his analysis of the change in the disposition over the means of military violence that occurs with the gradual breakdown of feudalism and the rise in and through war of the modern national bureaucratic state.[11]

A more detailed consideration of the impact of war on the structure of society raises the question whether centralization, cohesion and despotism, which Simmel seems to consider all part of one process, are indeed inseparable or whether they vary independently of each other. Simmel would of course be the first to recognize that these phenomena would also be affected by, among other things, the power relations and the general value structure of the society. A democratic tradition, for example, might limit to some extent the process of centralization.

Contrary to what Simmel implies, despotism—by which he apparently means absolute, irresponsible and autocratic control —does not follow necessarily in the wake of war. Whether despotism results from war situations is indeed largely dependent upon the degree of cohesion of the social system. But the relation that holds here seems to be the reverse of that implied by Simmel: it is not when social cohesion increases, but rather when cohesion is weak, when there is little "willing acceptance of authority" because of the weakness of internal solidarity, that "despotism" would be a prerequisite for meeting the war situation. Despotism appears to vary not in direct, but in inverse proportion to internal cohesion. The authoritarian regimes of modern Europe were all instituted in the wake of a serious loss of internal cohesion bordering on anomie. The established institutional order had disintegrated to a large extent; routines, expectations and role obligations had broken down.

On the other hand, if the basic social structure is stable, if basic values are not questioned, cohesion is usually strengthened by war through challenge to, and revitalization of, values and goals which have been taken for granted.

Interesting confirmation comes from a sociologist *qui s'ignore*, Winston Churchill, in an account of World War I and its aftermath: "The former peace-time structure of society had been . . . superseded and life had been raised to a strange intensity by the war spell. Under that mysterious influence, men and women had been appreciably exalted above death and pain and toil. Unities and comradeships had become possible between men and classes and nations and grown stronger while the hostile pressure and the common cause endured."[12]

Returning to a more general consideration of the effect of conflict upon group structures, we recall that conflict makes group members more conscious of their group bonds and increases their participation. Outside conflict has the same effect: it also mobilizes the group's defenses among which is the reaffirmation of their value system against the outside enemy.

Here the concept of "negative reference group," which Newcomb, refining Sumner's concept of "out-group," has introduced, would seem helpful.[13] Behavior will be influenced both by positive reference groups (those groups that are emulated or imitated) and by negative reference groups (those groups that provide motivations for opposing them). We discussed in the first proposition how such negative reference groups operate in the creation and integration of new groups such as classes. What Simmel asserts here is, then, simply a corollary of the earlier proposition: negative reference groups which lead, by calling forth opposition, to the formation of new groups, also lead, through conflict, to their further integration.

Charles H. Cooley neatly summed up this process when he wrote: "You can resolve the social order into a great number of co-operative wholes of various sorts, each of which includes conflicting elements within itself, upon which it is imposing some sort of harmony with a view to conflict with other wholes."[14] Freud makes a similar observation: "Hatred against a particular person or institution might operate in just the same unifying way, and might call up the same kind of emotional ties as positive attachment."[15]

However, strong group cohesion as a consequence of outside conflict does not necessarily carry with it the need for centralized control. Relevant at this point is our earlier questioning of Simmel's lumping together of warfare with other forms of conflict. Although in differentiated groups every type of conflict, whether peaceful or warlike, is likely to lead to further differentiation and also centralization, it is not possible to say the same about less differentiated groups. "Subordination implies cohesion, but not vice versa."[16] Indeed, a sect, engaged in intense conflict with the surrounding world of the "damned," may have such strong cohesion that each member of the group participates in the exercise of control tasks and that there is no need for centralization of these tasks in the hands of a few. The situation is different, however, once sects engage in *warfare* with the outside. As the history of English Puritanism before and during the Civil War illustrates vividly, once the "elect" actually fight the outside by force of arms, they develop differentiated structures required by the needs of warfare, and in turn this differentiation requires a measure of centralization of control tasks.

If a sect is defined as a body of "elect" which through conflict sets itself off from the main body of the larger religious group, we may expect that such separation will carry in its wake a high degree of internal cohesion. Whereas the Church is inclusive, the sect is exclusive. Exclusion is attained through conflict with the outside and the maintenance of this exclusive standing requires the sect to be an internally cohesive conflict group.[17] However, we cannot equate this internal cohesion with centralization. A great number of sects, most Protestant sects included, exhibit considerably less centralization than the larger church organization from which they seceded. Centralization and internal cohesion vary independently of each other.[18]

In sects and similar groups which do not require much differentiation of functions (where the division of labor remains on a rudimentary level), internal solidarity can to a large extent fulfill the group-integrating functions which in more differentiated groups are fulfilled by more developed authority structures.[19]

Of course, whenever a sect engages in warfare, it will indeed tend to centralize its organization. Whereas in other types of conflict all group members can possibly participate equally, the techniques of modern warfare require differentiation of functions and the emergence of a centralized structure.[20] A group engaged in warfare under modern conditions needs a general staff. This distinguishes most religious sects from the Bolshevik Party, although, as we have seen, they are similar in many other respects. The warlike sect, actively engaged in civil war or preparation for civil war, must differentiate its tasks in order to struggle effectively, and in continued struggle will feel the need for further differentiations and hence centralization. The history of the Bolshevik Party from its early inception to the party structure that finally emerged after the civil war details this process.

Outside conflict unites the group and heightens morale, but whether it will also result in centralization depends on the structure of the group itself as well as on the nature of the conflict.[21] Internal cohesion is likely to be increased in the group which engages in outside conflict. The occurrence of despotism, however, is inversely related to the strength of internal cohesion; despotism will occur where there is insufficient cohesion at the outset of the conflict and where the conflict situation fails to bring about the cohesion necessary for concerted action.

However, conflict between groups or nations has often led to anomie rather than to an increase in internal cohesion. This alternative sequence to which Simmel alludes needs to be incorporated in the present discussion.

The degree of group consensus prior to the outbreak of the

conflict seems to be the most important factor affecting cohesion. If a group is lacking in basic consensus, outside threat leads not to increased cohesion, but to general apathy, and the group is consequently threatened with disintegration. Research on the impact of the depression on the family has shown, for example, that families lacking internal solidarity before the depression responded apathetically and were broken, whereas solidary families actually were strengthened.[22]

Lack of consensus or lack of solidarity is not synonymous with divergencies and conflicts within the group. If the group reacts to outside threat by inner divergencies over the conduct of the conflict, it indicates that the issue at stake is important enough for the group members to fight about among themselves. This is quite different from the situation in which the members simply do not care about and remain indifferent to the outside threat.

Here a distinction introduced by Robin Williams seems to be most helpful:

> Given a social group which is a "going concern," a sensed outside threat *to the group as a whole* will result in heightened internal cohesion. . . . However [this general principle] holds true only under very specific conditions: (a) the group must be a "going concern," i.e., there must be a minimal consensus among the constituent individuals that the aggregate is a group, and that its preservation as an entity is worthwhile; (b) there must be recognition of an outside threat which is thought to menace the group as a whole, not just some part of it.[23]

The relation between outer conflict and inner cohesion does not hold true where internal cohesion before the outbreak of the conflict is so low that the group members have ceased to regard preservation of the group as worthwhile, or actually see the outside threat to concern "them" rather than "us." In such cases disintegration of the group, rather than increase in cohesion, will be the result of outside conflict.

The contrasting effects of the recent war on the French and on the British social structure provide a convenient illustration. The Nazi attack appreciably increased the internal cohesion of the British social system, temporarily narrowing the various political, social and economic fissures that existed in British society. In France, on the other hand, these fissures were widened to the point of a breakdown in consensus even concerning the most basic question of all: whether France was to continue as an independent national unit.

In discussing Simmel's proposition that internal conflict may be taken as an index of the stability of a relation, we made the distinction between conflicts that take place within a structure of consensual agreement and conflicts in which no such agreement exists. We concluded that only in the former case may internal conflict be said to be functional for the relation. We can now make the same point regarding the effect of outside conflict on inner structure: during World War II, attempts at centralization by the French government were unavailing and could not mend the basic cleavages nor remedy the lack of social solidarity. The only alternative to disintegration then came to be the "despotism" of the Pétain regime.

As long as the outside threat is perceived to concern the entire group (or society), internal conflicts do not hinder concerted action against the outside enemy. Negro-white relations in America exemplify this situation. The fact that the Negro minority, despite its exclusion from important rights and privileges of American society, showed no willingness during the Second World War to follow Japanese propaganda for "solidarity between the dark and yellow races" indicates that on the whole the Negro group did not abandon its identification with American values. On the contrary, one result of the war seems to have been an increase in Negro-white solidarity. External conflict had an integrative rather than a disruptive effect. On the other hand, enemy attack against British and Dutch colonies in southeast Asia resulted in disintegration of the social structure; a majority of the members of these societies perceived the threat as directed against "them," i.e., against the British or Dutch overlords, rather than as directed against "us," the natives. Because they did not define the situation as threatening to themselves, they were unresponsive to attempts to overcome the menace.

We may now reformulate Simmel's proposition:

Conflict with another group leads to the mobilization of the energies of group members and hence to increased cohesion of the group. Whether increase in centralization accompanies this increase in cohesion depends upon both the character of the conflict and the type of group. Centralization will be more likely to occur in the event of warlike conflict and in differentiated structures requiring marked division of labor.

Despotism seems to be related to lack of cohesion; it is required for carrying out hostilities where there is insufficient group solidarity to mobilize energies of group members.

In groups engaged in struggle with an external enemy, the occurrence of both centralization and of despotism depends upon the system of common values and upon the group structure prior to the outbreak of the conflict.

Social systems lacking social solidarity are likely to disintegrate in the face of outside conflict, although some unity may be despotically enforced.

Remembering a previous proposition which stated that the closer the relationship, the more intense the conflict, we are now led to ask whether outside conflict, given that it forces the group to pull itself together, does not thereby increase the possibility of the emergence of hostile feelings within the struggling group itself, and does not affect, consequently, the way in which this group deals with internal conflict. This relation will be examined presently.

PROPOSITION 10:

Conflict with Another Group Defines
Group Structure and Consequent Reaction
to Internal Conflict

"Groups in any sort of war situations are not tolerant. They cannot afford individual deviations from the unity of the coordinating principle beyond a definitely limited degree.

"The technique for this is sometimes an apparent tolerance. . . . The Catholic Church attained the close unitary front it needed . . . by treating dissenters as long as possible as belonging to it, but the moment this was not possible any longer, expelling them with incomparable energy. For group structures of this sort, a certain elasticity of their form is of the greatest importance. . . .

"A relatively small fighting group, in a situation of acute conflict, may benefit from a decline in its membership, as long as this decline purifies it of elements which tend to mediation and compromise. . . . The majority group does not have to insist on such decisiveness of pro and con. Vacillating and conditional members are less dangerous to it because . . . its large volume can afford such peripheral phenomena without being affected in its center. But where, as in the smaller group, the periphery is closer to the center, every uncertainty of a member at once threatens the core and hence the cohesion of the whole. The slight span between the elements makes for the absence of that elasticity of the group which here is the condition of tolerance."[24]

Simmel here makes clear what we have indicated previously, namely, that the violence of a group's reaction toward inner dissensions depends upon certain aspects of group structure as well as upon the intensity of the conflict situation.

Although groups which are under attack from the outside cannot afford to be "tolerant"[25] of internal dissent, they will handle it in varying ways. These different ways cannot be freely chosen. The group's reaction to internal dissent is related to certain aspects of its structure.

An analogy will clarify these structural differences: There are two ways in which a vessel can be made to withstand the pressure of surrounding water; either the hull may be made rigid and inelastic so that it resists great pressure, or it may be made flexible so that it can give way to some pressure without breaking under it. Simmel suggests that large organizations, such as the Catholic Church or major political parties, may adopt the second method, while smaller religious bodies, such as sects and minority political parties, may adopt the first. Each way of meeting an outside threat contains a special danger: too much rigidity may lead to splits and withdrawals; too much flexibility may lead to a blurring of boundaries and dissolution in the surrounding environment.

However correct Simmel's observation concerning group size may be, it is important to note that size is not an independent variable. Simmel tends to equate size of group with degree of involvement of its members. Although there is much evidence to suggest that the smaller the group the greater the involvement of the participants, since interaction among a few members tends to be more intense than interaction among many, we cannot assume that this relation holds invariably. A small-town Chamber of Commerce may have few members and still resemble a large Chamber of Commerce in the segmental involvement of its members. We must therefore distinguish between two aspects of group structure: (1) the numerical size of the group and (2) the degree of involvement of group members—although generally we can expect a simultaneous variation of these two factors.

Following Simmel's lead, let us examine how size and involvement are directly related to external conflict.

A historical example will help to illustrate the relation between the two aspects of group structure mentioned above and outside conflict, actual or expected.

The 1903 schism between Mensheviks and Bolsheviks, which was to have such momentous repercussions for modern history, occurred over what would appear to be a minor point in Party statutes. Two drafts lay before the delegates. Lenin's draft read as follows: "A member of the Russian Social-Democratic Workers Party is any person who accepts its program, supports the party with material means and *personally participates* in one of its organizations." The opposing draft, written by the leader of the Mensheviks, Martov, substituted for the last part of Lenin's formulation *"personally and regularly co-operates under the guidance* of one of its organizations."

At the time, what appeared to be mere hairsplitting actually involved a totally different conception of the structure of the party.[26] Lenin's conception can be traced back to the year 1900, when he wrote: "We must train people who shall devote to the party not only their spare evenings, but the whole of their lives."[27] Two years later he formulated his view more precisely: what the organization needed above all was a dedicated group of professional revolutionaries: "In a country *with a despotic government*, the more we *restrict* the membership of this organization to persons who are engaged in revolution as a profession, the more difficult it will be to catch the organization. . . . We can never give a mass organization that degree of secrecy which is essential. . . . The thing we need is a militant organization of agents. . . ."[28]

The political organization conceived by Lenin is similar to the organization of religious sects. The sect is "an association of religiously qualified, not like the Church a compulsory association for the administration of grace, which sheds its light over the just and the unjust and which attempts precisely to take the sinner especially under the discipline of divine law. The sect has the ideal of the 'ecclesia pura,' the visible community of saints, from the midst of which the black sheep have been thrown out so that they do not offend the eye of God." "The community [of the sect] constitutes a mechanism of selection, which separates the qualified from the non-qualified. . . ."[29]

Lenin's theory of organization and Weber's characterization of the sect both emphasize the formation of *ex*clusive bodies, the establishment of religious or political elites. These do not aspire to encompass the mass of men, but restrict themselves to attracting a special class of "performers."[30]

Lenin justified the need for the elite type of party in terms of the acute conflict situation which the revolutionary organization faced in its struggle against autocratic Czardom. As a fighting group it would have to relinquish the advantage of large numbers (Lenin did not, of course, deny that there was an advantage in larger numbers) in order to maintain the essential purity which the struggle required. Quite similar considerations had a part in the early formation of Protestant sects. They also were engaged in a harsh struggle with competing creeds bent on the destruction of heresy, so that the maintenance of the "purity" of the membership was of central importance.[31]

The Menshevik conception of organization also confirms the view that numerical size and membership involvement are related to the conflict situation that the group faces or expects to face. The Menshevik Party, or at least many of its most prominent representatives, did not expect increased conflict with Czardom, but rather decreasing conflict through gradual liberalization of the regime. Should the regime develop into a modified replica of Western democratic regimes, then surely there would be less need for an elite party. So, in accordance with this expectation, the organization should attract as many people as possible in order, when the time came, to compete for votes on the electoral market.

In other words, the Mensheviks, expecting a decrease in outside conflicts, contemplated a mass organization, a "church," an elastic organization tolerant of divergent tendencies, where dissenters would not be pushed into the ranks of heretics or renegades. Moreover, such an organization could admit men who, should they remain outside of the organization, might turn into rivals and competitors. Its strength would lie in the co-optation of dissenting elements, not in their exclusion.[32]

Social-Democratic parties, in Russia as well as in the rest of Europe, were cohesive organizations exhibiting strong internal solidarity. The large membership of these parties made possible, indeed necessary, the coexistence of different factions and alignments within the organization. In these groups (as we noted earlier about total societies) the crisscrossing of various internal conflicts, far from loosening the basic relationship, actually sewed the group together.

The situation is quite different, however, in small groups oriented toward continuous, acute conflict with the outside. For such groups, every internal dissension appears to endanger the mobilization of concerted energies for the outside conflict. Such groups cannot afford toward their members the leniency of larger groups. Insofar as relatively small size of such elite groups does mean total involvement of the members' personalities, what we said earlier about the reinforcing effect of affective involvement in conflict situations applies here: in groups in which the total personalities of members are involved, internal conflict becomes more readily imbued with nonrealistic elements. Then internal conflict would go so deep that it would touch directly the consensual basis of group structure. No dissent can therefore be tolerated, and the dissenter must be forced to withdraw. As Simmel asserted elsewhere: if the relationship allows no room for the assertion of conflicting attitudes, withdrawal is the only way out. Lenin's party was indeed continually torn by factional struggles leading to repeated splits and exclusions. Yet Lenin, far from deploring this outcome, insisted on the contrary that it would further strengthen the organization by increasing cohesion among the remaining members.

Whereas the church-type group strengthens its inner cohesion by allowing various conflicting tendencies to exist within its ranks, the political or religious sect must continuously expel dissenters to maintain or increase cohesion among the remaining "worthy" participants.

Once the group defines its structure according to its expectation of outside conflict, its response to inner dissent is no longer a matter of choice, but is determined by this very definition. In an earlier proposition we discussed the fact that the heretic calls forth violent hostility from his former associates not only because of the strength of previous affective identifications, but also because he symbolically, if not always in reality, threatens the very existence of his former group. We mentioned incidentally then that the reaction against heresy is likely to vary with the degree of outside conflict and so tends to be especially violent in groups engaged in acute conflict with the outside. We may now push this point further: a group that, from its inception, is conceived as a struggle group is especially prone to engage in violent heresy-hunting; and its members are obliged to participate continuously in the selection and reselection of those who are "worthy," that is, those who do not question or dissent, precisely because its very existence is based on the "purity" of its membership. Such groups must continuously engage in self-purification drives, and so they must constantly breed heresy and schisms.

Incessantly engaged in struggle with the outside and providing for no room for internal conflict, these groups will react violently not only against the heretic, but also against every form of dissent as an attack upon the very basis of the group's existence. The dissenter, unlike the heretic or the renegade, has not left the group either to join the ranks of an enemy or to set up a rival group of his own. Whereas the church-type group affords him expression within the structure, the sect sees in him only a potential "renegade."

We had occasion previously to point to the difference between the heretic and the renegade. We then said that the heretic is apt to create more confusion in the group than the renegade, for in his conflict with the group he still maintains the group's basic values, thereby threatening to blur its boundaries. We may now add that the dissenter creates even more confusion than the heretic who has left the group, for he claims belongingness. In small, struggling and close groups, the dissenter who still claims belongingness threatens to break up the group from within, for he does not represent to it the clear-cut danger of the heretic or apostate, against whom the group may find it easier to act concertedly. The dissenter is unpredictable and creates confusion: Will he go over to the enemy? Or does he intend to set up a rival group? Or does he intend to change the group's course of action? His fellow-members can be sure only that he is "up to something." By attacking the unanimity of group feelings he obtrudes an element of personal choice into a structure which is based upon unanimity of choice.

The small, close, struggling group will thus react instantly against the dissenter. The continuance of the group appears possible only by his forced or voluntary withdrawal.[33]

Once the group is a going concern, its structure helps to define its relation to conflict situations. Simmel has pointed this out most succinctly elsewhere, stressing that "radicalism" stemming from structure may be independent of radicalism as ideological content:[34]

> In general, small groups are more radical than large ones, whereby, of course, the ideas that form the basis of the party itself put the limits on its radicalism. Radicalism here is sociological in its very nature. It is necessitated by the unreserved devotion of the individual to the rationale of the group against other nearby groups (a sharpness of demarcation required by the need for the self-preservation of the group), and by the impossibility of taking care of widely varying tendencies and ideas within a narrow social framework. Of all this, the radicalism of *content* is largely independent.[35]

We now arrive at a reciprocal relationship between group structure and outside conflict. Simmel shows here that group structure helps to define the intensity of actual or expected conflict with the outside; and, as we have just seen, actual or expected intensity of external conflict in turn exerts pressure toward numerical smallness and high membership involvement. The small struggle group with high involvement will tend rigidly to maintain its ideological purity. In relatively larger, more inclusive groups, where members are not as deeply involved, ideological content is allowed to change in response to diverging and conflicting internal tendencies.

A large group that permits expression of dissent, and hence conflict, within its ranks draws its strength and cohesion from its flexibility. Cohesion, far from suffering in the process of such internal conflict, is strengthened by it. The small, close, struggle group, on the other hand, cannot deal with internal conflict and hence punishes expression of dissent with exclusion. Thus the close group, like a society that suppresses realistic group conflict, tends to produce scapegoating reactions. Not only does such a group define any actual dissent as "enemy activity," but it tends in addition to "invent" both inside and outside enemies in order to strengthen its inner solidarity. Such a group searches incessantly for an enemy, since its cohesion and its existence depend on him. We will pursue this point further in the following proposition.

In the foregoing discussion we identified two aspects of group structure which Simmel neglected to separate: (1) relative size; (2) degree of the members' involvements. We found that these must be considered in relation to a third, situational aspect: continuously struggling as against only occasionally struggling groups. We found that these aspects tend to occur in clusters; in other words, groups that are set up in the expectation of intense and continued outside conflict tend to be relatively small in size and to claim the allegance of the total personality of their members, and the converse is the case with large groups. While we have not examined all eight possible combinations of size, intensity of outside conflict, and degree of involvement, we can at least assert that a tendency exists for these aspects to cluster, resulting in the emergence of the two opposed types of group structure here discussed.

With these distinctions in mind, we may now reformulate Simmel's proposition:

Groups engaged in continued struggle with the outside tend to be intolerant within. They are unlikely to tolerate more than limited departures from the group unity. Such groups tend to assume a sect-like character: they select membership in terms of special characteristics and so tend to be limited in size, and they lay claim to the total personality involvement of their members. Their social cohesion depends upon total sharing of all aspects of group life and is reinforced by the assertion of group unity against the dissenter. The only way they can solve the problem of dissent is through the dissenter's voluntary or forced withdrawal.

Groups of the church type, not involved in continuous struggle with the outside, tend to make no special claims on the total involvement of the personality of the membership and, because they set up no rigid criteria for membership, are more likely to be large. Such groups are able to resist outside pressures successfully by exhibiting elasticity of structure and allowing an area of "tolerated conflict" within.

PROPOSITION 11:

The Search for Enemies

"Groups, and especially minorities, which live in conflict and persecution, often reject approaches or tolerance from the other side. The closed nature of their opposition without which they cannot fight on would be blurred. . . . A group's complete victory over its enemies is thus not always fortunate. . . . Victory lowers the energy which guarantees the unity of the group; and the dissolving forces, which are always at work, gain hold. . . . Within certain groups, it may even be a piece of political wisdom to see to it that there be some enemies in order for the unity of the members to remain effective and for the group to remain conscious of this unity as its vital interest."[36]

Following up the idea that outside conflict increases group cohesion, Simmel now claims that struggle groups may actually "attract" enemies in order to help maintain and increase group cohesion. Continued conflict being a condition of survival for struggle groups, they must perpetually provoke it.

Moreover, he implies, outside conflict need not even be objectively present in order to foster in-group cohesion; all that is necessary is for the members to perceive or be made to perceive an outside threat in order to "pull themselves together."[37] Threats may or may not exist in objective reality, but the group must feel that they do. Social perception of an outside threat may be distorted, but its effect on the in-group may be the same as that of undistorted perception of objective threat.

A struggle group's search for new enemies resembles the process that Gordon W. Allport has called "the functional autonomy of motives."[38] Allport contends that motives which have arisen originally in pursuit of a specific goal may continue to operate although the original goal no longer exists. Robert K. Merton uses a similar conceptual framework to explain bureaucratic ritualism with its characteristic displacement of goals, whereby "an instrumental value becomes a terminal value."[39] Likewise, conflict, which the group originally engaged in as a means to a stated end, now becomes an end in itself.

This recalls our earlier discussion of nonrealistic conflict. Just as such a conflict is governed not by the desire to obtain results, but by a need to release tension in order to maintain the structure of the personality, so the group's search for enemies is aimed not at obtaining results for its members, but merely at maintaining its own structure as a going concern.

Even after the initial conflict situation which brought them into being no longer prevails, struggle groups continue to act according to the "law upon which they originally entered the scene." As Chester Bernard says, "An organization must disintegrate if it cannot accomplish its purpose. It also destroys itself by accomplishing its purpose."[40] Thus new purposes must be found in order to avoid dissolution. The history of the Populist and Progressive farm movements in the United States shows many instances when farmers' organizations originally set up to combat railroad or elevator interests moved on, once this battle was won, to raise new demands and tackle other antagonists in the political sphere. In his study of the Canadian Commonwealth Federation in Saskatchewan, Seymour Lipset shows that the farmers' victory over a particular antagonist, far from leading to the disappearance of the struggle organization, led it to extend its field of operation against other antagonists.[41] Labor history also affords many similar examples.

Disappearance of the original enemy leads to a search for new enemies so that the group may continue to engage in conflict, thereby maintaining a structure that it would be in danger of losing were there no longer an enemy.[42]

We should stress here that the "new enemy" which these groups actually evoke, or whose threat they exaggerate, really exists, unlike the "invented" enemy we shall deal with later. Moreover, provoking the enemy by proclaiming his "dangerous intentions" may have the effect of a "self-fulfilling prophecy": the "enemy" will "respond" and in this way actually become as dangerous to the group as it accused him of being in the first place.

It would be rewarding to study the evolution of conflict groups from this point of view. Attention would focus on groups that have accomplished their original objective either through their own victory or because social change has brought about, without their intervention, the objective for which they originally struggled. The task would be to discover why some of these groups disappeared while others succeeded in finding other "hate objects" to maintain them.

Such "searching for the outside enemy" (or exaggeration of the danger which an actual enemy represents) serves not only to maintain the structure of the group, but also to strengthen its cohesion when threatened by a relaxation of energies or by internal dissension. Sharpness of outside conflict revives the alertness of the membership, and either reconciles divergent tendencies or leads to concerted group action against the dissenter.

The corollary of the "search for the outer enemy" is the search for the inner enemy when these rigid structures encounter defeat or an unexpected increased external danger.

Groups tend to deny that reverses in conflict with out-groups can be attributed to the strength of the adversary, for this would be an admission of their own weakness. Hence they look in their own ranks for a "dissenter" who hampered unity and the concerted action against the enemy. (Note the reaction against Menshevists, Trotskyists, and Bucharinists in the Bolshevik Party.) So in societies, where the rigidity of structure inhibits realistic conflict, a perennial tendency exists to account for defeat in war in terms of "treason" within. The "stab-in-the-back" myth was used by German nationalists after the First World War; it appeared again in Vichy's explanations for the defeat of France in the Second World War. This is a variant of the scapegoating mechanism: though defeat was due to outsiders, the violence of the reaction aroused looks for hate objects among insiders. Those group members who must bear the burden of being the scape-goats, through their sacrifice, cleanse the group of its own fail-ings, and in this way re-establish its solidarity: the loyal mem-bers are reassured that the group as a whole has not failed, but only some "traitors"; moreover, they can now reaffirm their righteousness by uniting in action against the "traitors." In strug-gle groups the same mechanism is at work in the perennial drives for purification, namely the "pulling together" of the group against an inner "threat."

The inner enemy who is looked for, like the outer enemy who is evoked, may actually exist: he may be a dissenter who has opposed certain aspects of group life or group action and who is considered a potential renegade or heretic. But the inner enemy also may be "found," he may be simply invented, in order to bring about through a common hostility toward him the social solidarity which the group so badly needs.

This mechanism may also operate in the search for the outer enemy: he may be invented to bring about social solidarity. W. I. Thomas' theorem that "if men define their situations as real, they are real in their consequences," would apply to the invention of enemies even more directly than to the search for a real enemy. If men define a threat as real, although there may be little or nothing in reality to justify this belief, the threat is real in its consequences—and among these consequences is the increase of group cohesion.

But the aspect of the scapegoating mechanism which concerns us more particularly here is the type of imaginary threat that the scapegoat represents. The anti-Semite justifies his persecution of the Jew in terms of the Jew's power, aggression and venge-fulness. "He sees in the Jew everything which brings him misery —not only his social oppressor but also his unconscious instincts."[43] Mingled fear and dread of the Jew is one of the key elements of the complex anti-Semitic syndrome. This imaginary threat leads to a "regrouping" of the anti-Semite by his joining, as in Germany, the real community of like-minded men, or by his joining, as in America, an imaginary pseudo-community of likewise threatened individuals. There comes about a kind of illusory collectivity of all those who are similarly "threatened" by the Jew and who have lost everything but their common "danger" in the face of the expected aggressive actions of Jews.

Some types of anti-Semitism, as do other forms of prejudice, have important functions for those who suffer from "degrouping," that is, from a loss of cohesion in the society of which they are a part. Anti-Semitism provides "a means for pseudo-orientation in an estranged world."[44] "The [Jew's] alienness seems to provide the handiest formula for dealing with the alienation of society."[45] The degrouped man, by directing his diffuse hostility upon a specific target and then attributing his sense of menace to this target group, attempts to find a solid point of repair in a world that otherwise makes no sense to him.

The "inner enemy" may be provided by the social system insofar as target selection is group-sustained and institutionalized. "Prejudice," as Talcott Parsons pointed out, "is not only directed by individuals against scapegoat groups, but can readily become a phenomenon of group attitude, that is, become partly institutionalized. Then instead of being disapproved by members of one's own group for being prejudiced, one is punished for not being prejudiced."[46] "Discrimination is sustained not only by the direct gains to those who discriminate, but also by cultural norms which legitimize discrimination."[47] There are indications that the degree of rigidity of the social structure may help determine the degree to which the acting out of prejudice (discriminatory behavior) against inner enemies is institutionalized. A few examples will clarify this point.

Writing just before the First World War, Thomas P. Bailey, a Mississippi professor, said of the association between fear of the Negro and the social status system of the South:

> The veriest slavery of the spirit is to be found in the deep-seated anxiety of the South. Southerners are afraid for the safety of their wives and daughters and sisters; Southern parents are afraid for the purity of their boys; Southern publicists are afraid that the time will come when large numbers of Negroes will try

to vote and thus precipitate race war. . . . Southern businessmen are afraid that agitation of the Negro question will interfere with business or demoralize the labor market. Southern officials are afraid of race riots, lynchings, savage atrocities, paying not only for Negro fiendishness but also for the anxiety caused by fear of what might be.[48]

More recent investigators have confirmed this early diagnosis. Frank Tannenbaum writes: "The South gives indications of being afraid of the Negro. I do not mean physical fear. It is not a matter of cowardice or bravery; it is something deeper and more fundamental. It is fear of losing grip upon the world."[49]

This pervasive fear among many Southerners of the Negro's aggressive violence serves an important function in maintaining the rigid Southern status system. If the Negro is dangerous, if he is a perennial threat to the most intimate possessions of the white Southerner, it is crucially important to "keep him in his place"; in other words, to maintain the position and the cohesion of the dominant white status group. If the Negro is dangerous, then all those in the white group who attempt to befriend him can be effectively characterized as "renegades" endangering the very existence of the white group.

Regarding fear of intermarriage and miscegenation, Myrdal remarks:

What white people really want is to keep the Negroes in a lower status. "Intermarriage" itself is resented because it would be a supreme indication of "social equality," while the rationalization is that "social equality" is opposed because it would bring about "intermarriage."[50]

Fear of the Negro, far from deriving from the Negro's actual behavior, is a means of keeping the status system intact, of rallying all members of the white group around its standards.[51]

To our knowledge, what we have said here about the relation between rigidity of structure and the search for the enemy still remains to be strictly verified, except on the level of small-group research.[52] But it seems to be a hypothesis well worth testing.

Thus, a study of the Communist Party would try to determine

to what extent external threats to the group are objectively real and to what extent, on the contrary, the membership must perpetually "create" external threats (or internal scapegoats) in order to maintain internal loyalty.

Similarly, it would be rewarding to study the internal cohesiveness of the Jewish and other religious minority groups from this point of view. It appears that anti-Semitism ordinarily increases the internal solidarity of the Jewish group,[53] but it may also be that social solidarity is strengthened by constant emphasis on the dangers of anti-Semitism whether or not it is actually present or objectively threatening at any particular time.

In line with the present discussion, we may reformulate Simmel's proposition:

Rigidly organized struggle groups may actually search for enemies with the deliberate purpose or the unwitting result of maintaining unity and internal cohesion. Such groups may actually perceive an outside threat although no threat is present. Under conditions yet to be discovered, imaginary threats have the same group-integrating function as real threats.

The evocation of an outer enemy or the invention of such an enemy strengthens social cohesion that is threatened from within. Similarly, search for or invention of a dissenter within may serve to maintain a structure which is threatened from the outside. Such scapegoating mechanisms will occur particularly in those groups whose structure inhibits realistic conflict within.

There are shifting gradations between the exaggeration of a real danger, the attraction of a real enemy, and the complete invention of a threatening agent.

The following chapters will turn from the relation between conflict and group structure to the consideration of the relationship between antagonists. This calls, first, for a study of the relation between intensity of conflict and the content of conflict, and then for an examination of the various forms of "unification" which conflict establishes between the contenders.

CHAPTER VI

IDEOLOGY AND CONFLICT

PROPOSITION 12:

Ideology and Conflict

"The parties' consciousness of being mere representatives of supra-individual claims, of fighting not for themselves but only for a cause, can give the conflict a radicalism and mercilessness which find their analogy in the general behavior of certain very selfless and very idealistically inclined persons. . . . Such a conflict which is fought out with the strength of the whole personality while the victory benefits the cause alone, has a noble character. . . . On the basis of this mutual agreement of the two parties, according to which each of them defends only his claims and his cause, renouncing all personal or egoistic considerations, the conflict is fought with unattenuated sharpness, following its own intrinsic logic, and being neither intensified nor moderated by subjective factors.

"The contrast between unity and antagonism is perhaps most visible where both parties really pursue any identical aim—such as the exploration of a scientific truth. Here any yielding . . . any peace prior to the wholly decisive victory would be treason against that objectivity for the sake of which the personal character has been eliminated from the fight. Ever since Marx, the social struggle has developed into this form . . . the personal bitterness of both general and local battles has greatly decreased. . . . The violence of the fight, however, has not decreased for that. On the contrary, it has become more pointed . . . owing to the consciousness of the individual involved that he fights not only for himself, and often not for himself at all, but for a great super-personal aim."[1]

WITH THIS PROPOSITION Simmel distinguishes between two types of conflict: that in which the goal is personal and subjective and that in which the object of contention has an impersonal, objective quality.

Simmel's remarks bear upon two distinct consequences of the objectification of conflict: (1) the collective aim, transcending personal interests, will make the struggle more intense; (2) a unifying element exists between the contending parties in their adherence to the common norm of abstention from personal attacks. In other words, the present proposition concerns (1) the effect of objectification upon the intensity of the conflict, and (2) the effect of objectification upon the relation between the antagonists.

Simmel claims that objectified struggles, which transcend the personal, are likely to be more radical and merciless than conflicts over immediately personal issues. The consciousness of speaking for a superindividual "right" or system of values reinforces each party's intransigence, mobilizing energies that would not be available for mere personal interests and goals. He bases this assertion on two arguments: (1) that individuals entering into a superindividual conflict act as *representatives* of groups or ideas; and (2) that they are imbued with a sense of *respectability* and self-righteousness since they are not acting for "selfish" reasons.

Yet the second of these arguments, that people engaged in a conflict which transcends their individual interests fight more forcefully because they are not bound by norms of "personal reserve," does not seem to hold true universally. In an institutional order wherein self-interest and "success" are highly approved, self-interest is not devoid of superpersonal and moral significance. Far from being defined as opposed to the goals of the collectivity, self-interested behavior, at least that according with the social definitions of certain roles, is regarded as morally desirable and in accord with the expectations and value assumptions of the group.[2] The superior respectability of superindividual action may apply to Germany around the turn of the century when, owing to a still heavy admixture of feudal and noncapitalist elements in the value structure of the society, self-interest was not yet fully legitimized, especially in the eyes of those who belonged to the academic community. But the criterion of respectability does not universally distinguish an action pursued for subjective, self-interested reasons from one pursued for objective interests; both may indeed be equally "respectable." The real difference is whether self-interest is being pursued with a good or a bad conscience, in other words, whether its pursuit is considered legitimate by the actor himself and by the collectivity of which he is a part and from which he seeks approval.

It appears, then, that the grain of truth in Simmel's statement is that conflict pursued with a "good conscience" (as this has just been defined) is generally more radical and merciless than where such inner support is lacking. For example, one reason for the apparently decreased combativeness of American management in labor struggles today, as compared with fifty years ago, can perhaps be found in a decreased belief in the absolute righteousness of maximizing profits both in the society at large and in the business community itself.[3]

Whether the giving up of personal interest in favor of a collective orientation adds to the "respectability" of a conflict may thus be held to depend on whether individual success orientation is approved in the normative system.

But Simmel's essential distinction remains between conflict motivated by personal goals and that in which individuals enter as "representatives" of superindividual claims. Among the many roles an individual plays are "representative" roles, that is, roles in which he acts in the name of a collectivity to which he belongs. Parsons, who has coined the term, restricts it to leadership roles.[4] However, it may be fruitful to extend its use to describe the role of any member of a group who has outside-the-group relations in which he acts and is expected to act as its representative. In the Marxian labor movement, for example, any active member, whether or not he had a leadership role in the organization, was expected "to represent" the movement to the outside world.

The individual who is expected to act as a representative of his group sees himself as the embodiment of its purposes and of its power. He identifies with the group by making it a part of himself, by introjecting it, thus enriching and aggrandizing himself. His energies are thereby strengthened and his fight imbued with feelings of power derived from the power he ascribes to the collectivity.[5]

Not only does he make the group part of himself; he makes himself more fully part of the group by giving up personal claims for the sake of the group cause. As Kurt Lewin has pointed out,[6] making sacrifices for an organization increases loyalty to it.[7] The member who for the sake of the group relinquishes some of his immediate personal interests feels that he has invested in it; he has projected upon it part or all of his personality. Through introjection of the group's purpose and power and through projection of his own self into the group, the group has become but an extension of his own personality. Under these conditions, threats to the group touch the very core of his personality.

A struggle for a superindividual cause, being stripped of all individual (and hence differing) interests and desires, forces attention upon the one immediate purpose, thus concentrating all forces for concerted action in one direction. Individuals imbued with the feeling that they "represent" the group's purposes, that they *embody* it, will be all the more ready to respond to impersonal appeals.

Simmel's proposition calls special attention, then, to this distinction between conflict in which the participants engage as "private individuals" and conflict in which they engage as representatives of collectivities in which they have invested parts of their personalities. The second kind of conflict assumes a more intransigent character. The respectability of the lack of "self-interest," to which Simmel refers, is contingent upon the representative role. A culture oriented toward individual achievement still disapproves of the pursuit of self-interest in those areas in which individuals are expected to act in representative roles. The representative role sets a normative limit to the pursuit of self-interest even in a social system which is pervaded by an ethos of individual success.[8]

This notion of the representative role may now be related to the first proposition: that groups become increasingly aware of their specificity through conflict and in this way establish or maintain the boundaries between themselves and the outside. Part of what is meant by the concept of "group consciousness" (or class consciousness, as the case may be) is the transformation of individuals with their own specific life situations into conscious representatives of the group. The individual will be more intransigent in his representative role because he sees himself as the bearer of a group mission. Accommodation, which is permissible or even desirable on the level of personal behavior, is no longer permissible for the representative of group interests which transcend the "merely" personal.

In this context we see the sociological importance of Marx's famous rejection of the "personal element" in his criticism of capitalism: "I paint the capitalist and the landlord in no sense 'couleur rose.' But here individuals are dealt with only in so far as they are the personifications of economic categories, embodiments of particular class relations and class interests. My standpoint . . . can less than any other make the individual responsible for relations whose creature he socially remains, however much he may subjectively raise himself above them."[9] In this respect, Marx and Simmel are in accord: the class struggle is to be "depersonalized" so that the antagonists on both sides appear in their roles as representatives of the antagonistic camps. Only thus can the struggle achieve the intensity and intransigence which Marx advocates.[10] By insisting on the impersonal character of the class struggle, Marx sought to give the worker not only the feeling that he was fighting in accord with the "wave of the future," but also the feeling that different standards must be applied to his personal actions than to his actions as a representative of class interests and class organization.

Simmel's observation that struggle is intensified through the depersonalizing of its purpose throws light on one aspect of the intellectual's role in social issues. Intellectuals have been of central importance in "objectifying" social movements, in transforming them from interest groups into ideological movements. Marx himself was, of course, a preeminent and characteristic example of the intellectual who, in Karl Mannheim's words, perpetually transforms conflicts of interest into conflicts of ideas. Intellectuals have contributed to the deepening and intensification of struggles by stripping them of their personal motivations and transforming them into struggles over "eternal truths."[11]

It is precisely this function of the intellectuals which has earned them the enmity of those theoreticians of the American labor movement who are concerned with confining conflicts to immediate issues rather than extending them into political and ideological spheres. In his passionate defense of the traditional pragmatism of the American labor movement and his rejection of objectification through Marxian goals and strategy, Selig Perlman writes: "It has always been the main characteristic of the intellectual to think of labor as an abstract 'mass' in the grip of an abstract 'force.'" "Labor then ceases to be an aggregation of individuals seeking as a group to control their common economic opportunity. Instead, labor takes on the aspect of a 'mass' driven by a 'force' towards a glorious 'ultimate goal.'" "At bottom, the intellectual's conviction rests . . . on a deeply rooted faith that labor is somehow the 'chosen vessel' of whatever may be the power which shapes the destiny of society."[12] Elsewhere Perlman goes on to indicate that the "abstraction" from everything specific and immediate leads to an intensified struggle. Joseph Schumpeter's attack on the role of intellectuals in the labor movement also becomes understandable here: "Intellectuals," Schumpeter says, "verbalized the movement, supplied theories and slogans for it . . . made it conscious of itself and in so doing changed its meaning. . . . They naturally radicalized it, eventually imparting a revolutionary bias to the most bourgeois trade-union practices."[13]

Other examples than those concerning the labor movement could readily be adduced for illustrating this aspect of the role of intellectuals in intensifying conflict. Much research must be done before sociologists can say with any assurance under which conditions intellectuals, by providing and systematizing the ideology of a movement and thereby giving it collective orientation, have played a central part in the ideological transformation of movements and hence in deepening the conflicts of these movements with enemy strata and groups.

We must now consider Simmel's view that the common rejection of the "personal" between two parties to a conflict always constitutes a "unifying" element between them. It is immediately apparent that his examples refer, in fact, to two distinct types of conflict.

One of these types occurs when parties, in the pursuit of a common goal, struggle over the best means of achieving it. This is well illustrated by Simmel's example of a scientific controversy. The antagonists have in common the search for truth, and for both of them the quest and the standards by which it is to be pursued inhere in the methods and ethos of science and its institutionalized goal: the extension of certified knowledge.[14] Rival theoretical claims involve their protagonists in conflicts over possibly mutually exclusive interpretations, but conflict here not only involves a common point of reference and the acceptance of common rules, as in the cases to be discussed in the next chapter, but also a common goal.

Simmel also speaks of the conflict in which the "unifying" function lies not in the acceptance by both parties of a common goal and common methods of reaching it, but in the mere rejection by both of self-interested motivation and commitment of each to some superindividual cause. This case does not differ from the first one merely in degree, as Simmel implies. Actually, the effect of objectification here may be exactly the reverse of unifying: it draws a sharp line of distinction between the antagonists with the result that each is more likely to seek to defeat the other through intensive struggle. Here Simpson's criticism[15] seems to be valid: what is integrated primarily is each party within itself. A revolutionary labor movement committed to the overthrow of existing property relations and an entrepreneurial organization committed to their defense may both agree to reject "personal" arguments and animosities (one wonders, by the way, whether this has generally been the case), yet this "common ground" is of secondary importance since they "agree" on this point precisely in order to pursue their diametrically opposed aims.

If the objectification of which Simmel speaks leads to a breakdown of consensus, the "common element" in the conflict touches only superficial areas of the total relation. It consists only of the agreement to exclude certain methods of struggle, such as personal vilification. In the course of this, the struggle involves integration within each party partly in terms of rejecting the values and goals of the other.

In most conflicts, however, including those conducted for a superindividual cause, other binding elements are present or produced during the course of the conflict. Objectification is not a unifying factor unless it accompanies other binding elements, such as a common goal. The next chapter will discuss other "socializing factors" brought about by the conflict.

To reformulate Simmel's proposition:

Conflicts in which the participants feel that they are merely the representatives of collectivities and groups, fighting not for self but only for the ideals of the group they represent, are likely to be more radical and merciless than those that are fought for personal reasons.

Elimination of the personal element tends to make conflict sharper, in the absence of modifying elements which personal factors would normally introduce. The modern Marxian labor movement exemplifies the radicalizing effects of objectification of conflict. Strict ideological alignments are more likely to occur in rigid than in flexible adjustive structures.

Objectification of the conflict is likely to be a unifying element for the contending parties when both parties pursue the same purpose: for example, in scientific controversies in which the issue is the establishment of truth.

CHAPTER VII

CONFLICT—THE UNIFIER

PROPOSITION 13:

Conflict Binds Antagonists

"If . . . a fight simply aims at annihilation, it does approach the marginal case of assassination in which the admixture of unifying elements is almost zero. If, however, there is any consideration, any limit to violence, there already exists a socializing factor, even though only as the qualification of violence. Kant said that every war in which the belligerents do not impose some restrictions in the use of possible means upon one another, necessarily . . . becomes a war of extermination. It is almost inevitable that an element of commonness injects itself into . . . enmity once the stage of open violence yields to another relationship, even though this new relation may contain a completely undiminished sum of animosity between the two parties.

"One *unites* in order to fight, and one fights under the mutually recognized control of norms and rules."[1]

HERE SIMMEL MAKES TWO SEPARATE but related assertions. He says that the very act of entering into conflict with an antagonist establishes relations where none may have existed before. Conflict is seen as a binding element between parties that may previously have stood in no relation to each other. In addition, Simmel claims that conflict tends to give rise to regulations and norms governing its conduct and restraining the forms in which it is being fought out. Let us examine these assertions in turn.

By definition, engaging in conflict with another party means that a relationship with that party has been established. However, Simmel claims more than this. He implies that once relations have been established through conflict, other types of relations are likely to follow. Elsewhere in his essay, he maintains that "the mutual relations of primitive groups is almost always one of hostility," so that "in early stages of culture, war is almost the only form in which contact with alien groups is brought about at all." While this is certainly an overstatement in the light of more recent anthropological evidence,[2] war, both in its more primitive and its modern forms, is indeed one of the means of establishing contact between groups. War has often led (as, for example, Roman history and the history of modern imperialism amply demonstrate) to cross-fertilization of previously unrelated cultures and has established relations where none existed before.

Simmel of course was aware that wars have often resulted in all but complete destruction of one of the participants; thus some American Indian tribes and other aboriginal cultures were almost totally destroyed. He suggests only that warfare tends to lead to other forms of interaction except in those extreme circumstances where it approximates the attack of the thug upon his victim.

Although analogies between large-scale social phenomena such as war and comparatively less complex patterns of interaction are always hazardous, we feel justified here in pointing to similar processes in interpersonal relations. Child psychologists have pointed out that contention or conflict is often one way in which children engage in a relationship.[3] After first having quarreled over the use of a toy, children who previously were strangers to each other may proceed to play with it co-operatively. A child, having been tested in the conflict relationship, can now become a playmate.[4] Adult behavior offers many similar examples. Conflict seems to be one means of acquiring knowledge about an initially unknown person, thus establishing a basis for other forms of interaction.

Hostile interaction thus often leads to subsequent friendly interaction, conflict being a means to "test" and "know" the previously unknown. The stranger may become familiar through one's struggle with him.

Simmel's second assertion was that the mere fact of engaging in conflict brings about, except in marginal cases, the common acceptance of rules governing the conduct of hostilities. Such rules contribute to the socialization of the contending parties by imposing restraints on both of them.

In the first place, the very outbreak of conflict usually denotes that there exists a common object of contention. If there were no common interest in some object, there could scarcely be conflict since there would be nothing to fight about.[5]

In addition, Simmel asserts that conflict usually takes place within a common universe of norms and rules, and that it leads to the establishment or extension of such norms and rules. A conflict over the ownership of a piece of land implies that both parties to the conflict accept the idea of property rights and the general rules regarding the exercise of those rights. What they are fighting about is not the principle, but its application in the specific case. Property laws define the framework of the conflict, if not the concrete moves of the parties. Property laws, accepted in common by the parties, constitute a unifying bond between them.

Pertinent here is Durkheim's discussion of the "non-contractual element of contract."[6] Durkheim establishes that, even in purely "interested" market relations, "a contract is not sufficient unto itself but is possible only thanks to a regulation of the contract which is originally social."[7] Contractual relations are actually established in a context of norms that exist prior to, and are not specified in, the contract. The cohesive force implicit in a system of contractual relations derives, then, not from the mutual advantage of the parties to the transaction, but from the presence of an "organic solidarity" existing before the transaction is undertaken. Laws and customs both regulate contract; without them, contract, far from integrating society, would lead to disruptive strife.

As with contract, so, for Simmel, with conflict: it is generally fought within a universe of binding norms and thus carries with it the elements of its own limitation and regulation.[8] However, Simmel goes one step further. He implies that in the course of conflict new rules are continuously created and old rules modified. By bringing about new situations, which are partly or totally undefined by rules and norms, conflict acts as a stimulus for the establishment of new rules and norms.

At this point it might be well to consider, if only in passing, the rich literature on rules of warfare.[9] What we have said about the common universe of norms within which conflicts are generally fought seems inapplicable to warfare, in which the parties may have different or opposed institutions and norms. Yet attempts to limit the means of warfare are apparently as old as war itself. If both sides adhere to common rules, the conflict assumes predictability which it would otherwise lack. Both sides desire to rely on standards that allow them to calculate the consequences of their warlike acts. The rules of warfare tend to give rise to the notion of "limited liability," so that total destruction of the vanquished becomes unlikely. Regulations concerning prisoners of war have similar functions. The professional indoctrination of soldiers prior to the outbreak of a war instills in them respect for such rules so that, once engaged in combat, they will not overstep the bounds of what both parties consider suitable (predictable) behavior.

Continuous changes in the techniques of warfare create new situations requiring ever new rules. Consider the elaboration of rules concerning aerial bombing, germ warfare, gas warfare, and the like. Of course, rules are not always adhered to or readily accepted by contenders, as witness recent discussions over the use of atomic weapons. However, new warfare situations do exert pressure on the contenders to adopt a minimum of rules and norms, thus allowing them to make some estimate of the impact of new methods on the conduct of the conflict.

What has been said about war between culturally dissimilar contenders applies *a fortiori* to conflicts within a culture; they give rise to new norms and rules in new situations. K. N. Llewellyn and A. Adamson Hoebel illustrate this point in their study of conflict and case law in primitive jurisprudence: "It is the case of hitch or trouble," they write, "that dramatizes a 'norm' or a conflict of 'norms' which may have been latent. It forces conscious attention; it forces the defining of issues. . . . It forces solution, which may be creation. It forces solution in a fashion to be remembered, perhaps in clear, ringing words. It is one more experiment toward new and clearer and more rigorous patterning both of behavior and of recognized and recognizable 'norm' into that peculiarly legal something one may call a 'recognized imperative.' "[10] "For in any conflict situation—and conflict situations present the legal problem, par excellence—drive elicits challenge. And challenge forces conscious shaping of issues, conscious moves to persuade or to prevail by other means. . . . A trouble-case is dramatic, it is memorable; . . . its solution, once achieved, presses for repetition as few phenomena of life can press."[11]

Conflict, as seen here, revitalizes existent norms and creates a new framework of norms within which the contenders can struggle. In Max Weber's discussion of the sociology of law, a similar formulation occurs. Weber asks: "Wherefrom stems the 'new' element in customary law?" He states:

> One may answer that it is caused by changes in the external conditions of life which carry in their wake modifications of the empirically prevailing "consensual understanding." But the mere *change of external conditions* is neither sufficient nor necessary to explain the changes in the "consensual understandings." The really decisive element has always been a *new line of conduct* which then results either in a change of the meaning of the existing rules of law or in the creation of new rules of law. Several types of persons participate in these transformations. First . . . those individuals who are interested in some concrete communal action. Such an individual may change his behavior . . . either to protect his interests under new external conditions or simply to promote them more effectively under existing conditions. As a result there arise new "consensual understandings" and some-

times new forms of rational association with substantially new meanings; these, in turn, generate the rise of new customary behavior.[12]

Although Weber goes on to consider cases where new laws arise from other sources than the actions of individual participants, it is sufficient for our purpose to point out that Weber agrees that the clash of "interests" (understood in a general, not in an economic, sense) leads to the creation and modification of law.

These observations on the law-creating aspects of conflict apply more directly to Common Law than to other types of law. Dean Roscoe Pound, writing on Common Law, states: "The significant feature [of the method of judicial precedents] is reliance, for authoritative legal material, on judicial decision of actual controversies,"[13] and Walton H. Hamilton, discussing Judicial process, writes: "The character of the Judicial process is determined by the institution of litigation. . . . In the instance the suits are controlled by the rules; in the aggregate the rules are controlled by the suits."[14]

We need hardly document in detail the fact that legislative enactment of new statutory law tends to occur in areas in which conflict has pointed out the need for the creation of new rules. Any textbook on the legislative process or even reference to the daily newspaper provides ample documentation.

Fruitful investigation could be made of the relation between the incidence of industrial conflict and laws governing labor-management relations[15] or the relation between the occurrence of prison revolts and penal reform. The contribution Jehovah's Witnesses made to the redefinition of civil and religious liberties in the last decade by openly challenging a number of regulations and police edicts, needs to be more fully explored.

Conflicts may be said to be "productive" in two related ways: (1) they lead to the modification and the creation of law; (2) the application of new rules leads to the growth of new institutional structures centering on the enforcement of these new rules and laws.[16]

Simmel's proposition suggests a third unifying function of conflict, which is also indicated in the above quotation from Llewellyn and Hoebel: that conflict brings into the conscious awareness of the contenders and of the community at large, norms and rules that were dormant before the particular conflict.

Here another striking similarity emerges between the theories of Simmel and Durkheim. Durkheim, in his famous discussion of crime, maintains that crime is a "normal" phenomenon not only in that it is intimately linked with the basic conditions of social life, so that particular forms of violation of normative rules correspond to particular types of societies,[17] but also in that it is functional for the integration of all societies: "Crime brings together upright consciences and concentrates them."[18] By arousing the sentiments of the community on the consequences of infringement of rules, crime, according to Durkheim, contributes to the revival and maintenance of common sentiments; it is "a factor in public health, an integral part of all healthy societies."[19]

One has only to replace "crime," which may sometimes be a form of conflict, with "conflict" generally, to arrive at Simmel's meaning of the integrative function of antagonistic behavior.[20] Conflict, for Simmel, just as crime for Durkheim, brings out the need for the application of rules that, had no conflict occurred, might remain dormant and forgotten, like boundary stones between proprietors who have never quarreled over boundary lines. Those who engage in antagonistic behavior bring into consciousness basic norms governing rights and duties of citizens.[21] Conflict thus intensifies participation in social life. This very consciousness of the need for rules governing their behavior makes the contenders aware that they belong to the same moral universe.

According to some interpretations of Simmel's proposition, what actually binds the parties is not the conflict as such, but rather their shared values—so that integration must be accounted for by the common values rather than by the conflicting behavior. This is not a satisfactory interpretation.[22] Simmel shows that the binding values or norms are brought into awareness through conflict so that conflict, far from being only incidental to an affirmation of common values, is an agency through which these values come to be affirmed.

This discussion of the modification and creation of norms in and through conflict now enables us to see more clearly the reasons why conflict may be functional for societies. As we shall see shortly in greater detail, conflict is a mechanism through which adjustment to new conditions can be brought about. A flexible society benefits from conflict behavior inasmuch as this behavior, through the creation and modification of norms, assures its continuance under changed conditions. A rigid system, on the other hand, by not permitting conflict, will impede needed adjustments and so maximize the danger of catastrophic breakdown.

To reformulate Simmel's proposition:

Conflict may initiate other types of interaction between antagonists, even previously unrelated antagonists. It also usually takes place within a universe of norms prescribing the forms in which it is to be carried out. Conflict acts as a stimulus for establishing new rules, norms, and institutions, thus serving as an agent of socialization for both contending parties. Furthermore, conflict reaffirms dormant norms and thus intensifies participation in social life.

As a stimulus for the creation and modification of norms, conflict makes the readjustment of relationships to changed conditions possible.

PROPOSITION 14:

Interest in Unity of the Enemy

"In view of the incomparable utility of unified organization for purposes of fight, one would suppose every party to be extremely interested in the opposed party's lack of such unity. Nevertheless, there are some contrary cases. The centralized form into which the party is pushed by the situation of conflict grows beyond the party itself and causes it to prefer that the opponent, too, take on this form. In the struggles of the last decades between workers and employers, this has been most unmistakably the case."[23]

The previous proposition held that conflict tends to introduce a common element between the adversaries by submitting both of them to norms and regulations governing the struggle. Simmel now suggests that, since every party wishes the antagonist to act according to the same norms as its own, it may come to desire the unification or perhaps centralization of both itself and opponent. The paradox inherent in the desire for the opponent to have an advantageous form of organization is explained by Simmel: each contender wishes to deal with the adversary on the level of conflict techniques that he finds adequate for his own internal structure. It is difficult for a modern army to deal with the tactics of guerilla bands; a unified federated trade union finds it difficult to carry on conflicts with dispersed firms of small entrepreneurs. In addition, a contender may wish to see an antagonist as cohesive as he himself in order to facilitate the resolution of conflicts.

Even so, Simmel's position still contains elements of an unresolved paradox. It is obvious, and Simmel is cognizant of the fact, that a general who has a centralized army organization will not help his adversary to build a well-disciplined army before proceeding to overrun his country; nor will an unreconstructed entrepreneur help to build a unified labor organization in order to deal with his workers. The principle of divide and rule more often marks such situations. The proposition seems to be applicable only *insofar as there exists already a level of struggle in which the contending parties have reached a rough equality of strength.*

If a strongly organized adversary faces a weakly organized one, as in colonial wars or in labor-management relations before the advent of unionism, the strong will not be inclined to promote the unification of the weak. Similarly, in a totalitarian society the concentration of power on top requires the atomization rather than the unification of internal resistance. Where the adversary is viewed not as an opponent capable of engaging in potentially harmful *re*action, but as a powerless victim, Simmel's observation does not seem to apply.

If, however, there exists a rough balance of power, as in pluralistic, multi-group societies, the more strongly organized adversary may actually prefer that the weaker not fight with "unconventional weapons" (corresponding to a different organizational structure), but use weapons similar to his own, making it possible to fight according to comparable rules.

To evaluate and document this contention, we shall concentrate on the field of industrial relations. Other spheres, such as the strategy of warfare, appear to afford equally relevant illustrations.

There seems to be ample evidence that the unification of management tends to keep pace with the unification of unions, the two groups conditioning each other as outside conflict strengthens the cohesion of each.

As Frederick H. Harbison and Robert Dubin have remarked:

> Bigness on the side of industry leads to bigness on the side of organized labor. The reverse is also true. In the coal industry, for example, region-wide and later nation-wide pressure by the United Mine Workers made a strong employers' organization necessary for purposes of collective bargaining. In any industry where the business units are small and they face as a group the unified power of a strong international union, bargaining on a multi-employer basis is often the only means of *mutual* protection. . . . Bargaining between big unions and big corporations often leads to internal centralization of decision-making and policy determination on both sides.[24]

But what is more, Simmel's proposition suggests that the common universe of rules within which modern unions and modern management operate leads to the concern of each that the other live up to the rules even in conflict situations. This living up to the rules, however, requires unified and disciplined organization.

Thus we note that Samuel Gompers, the father of modern American labor organization, consistently favored the organization of employers. He stated: "We welcome the organization of the employers. We know one thing, that when there is organization founded upon a rational basis there is a greater tendency to agreement between the employers and the employed."[25] Similarly, it has recently been reported that German unions requested the American Military Government to allow reorganization of the employers' association, presumably to have someone with whom they could hope to bargain.[26]

As labor-management relations become formalized and routinized, each side will be concerned with restraining "unruly" members on the other side. This has happened frequently in recent years. C. Wright Mills quotes from contracts in which union leadership guarantees management against unauthorized strikes, so that "workers who follow unregulated militants, acting without due authority, are subject to penalties. To have no strikes is the responsibility of both company and union. They are disciplining agents for each other, and both discipline the malcontented elements among unionized employees."[27]

Agreement exists between union and management to protect the relationship against disturbances that unauthorized spokesmen would be likely to evoke. Either side will then be interested in the unified structure of the other.[28]

Also, unions seem often to agree that bargaining can be carried on more efficiently with organized employers. This explains why "in the overwhelming majority of instances . . . unions have not opposed or have even welcomed the formation of employers' associations, and *in some cases the employers have organized at the suggestion and with the help of the union*."[29] In a number of instances, for example in the garment industry, unions have forced employers to form associations so that the union might avoid bargaining with many different small employers.

This limited examination has shown the need for considering the circumstances under which Simmel's proposition would hold true.[30] The main qualification to be introduced is the one mentioned at the beginning of this discussion: each party is likely to desire the unification of the other only if a relative balance of strength is felt to exist between the parties. The distinction Mills makes between "practical" and "sophisticated" conservatives[31] seems to hinge on this qualification. The "sophisticated" conservative wing of American business, recognizing the power of unions, has accepted the necessity of living with them and hence desires that the unions' structure be similar to their own so that they can rely on a common universe of rules.[32] The "practical" conservatives still feel that no approximate balance of power exists between them and labor and that unions are weak enough so that they can be smashed.

This discussion has been limited to labor-management relations. It would seem applicable to other cases, for example to the relations between federal administrative agencies and their clients. It seems that bureaucratization of a group leads to a preference for the bureaucratization of its opponent. Philip Selznick's work on the TVA[33] documents abundantly the dilemma of an organization committed to a grass-roots, decentralized approach which, in its conflicts with regional and local adversaries, is forced to accommodate gradually to such centralized organizations as the American Farm Bureau Federation. Centralized and bureaucratic types of organizations will prefer to deal, both in conflict and in subsequent accommodation, with other bureaucratic organizations.

To reformulate Simmel's proposition:

In view of the advantages of unified organization for purposes of winning the conflict, it might be supposed that each party would strongly desire the absence of unity in the opposing party. Yet this is not always true. If a relative balance of forces exists between the two parties, a unified party prefers a unified opponent.

Labor unions have often preferred to deal with employers' associations rather than with individual employers. Although strikes might spread further and last longer in such cases, both parties prefer that the form of the conflict be in line with their own structural requirements. Only by dealing with representative organizations of employers can workers feel sure that the result will not be jeopardized by independent operators; and, correlatively, employers will tend to prefer to deal with unified labor organizations, which are able to control "unruly" or autonomous members. In opposing a diffuse crowd of enemies, one may more often gain isolated victories, but then one very rarely arrives at decisive results which fix a more enduring relationship. This explains the apparent paradox that each opponent may see the advantage of his enemy as his own advantage.

We noted earlier that continued engagement in conflict tends to bring about acceptance by both parties of common rules regulating the conduct of the conflict. We may now add that, under the conditions described, conflict also calls for a common organizational structure to facilitate the acceptance of common rules and conformity with them.

Since the aim of realistic conflict is to attain specific results, it follows that the contenders have no interest in pursuing it once such results have been attained. Centralization of the internal structure of each contending party assures that once these results are reached, peace can be concluded and maintained effectively as long as the same conditions prevail. This raises a further question: how can relative power, as the basis of peace, be assessed? We will discuss this question in the next proposition.

PROPOSITION 15:

Conflict Establishes and Maintains Balance of Power

"The most effective prerequisite for preventing struggle, the exact knowledge of the comparative strength of the two parties, is very often attainable only by the actual fighting out of the conflict."[34]

Simmel here appears to advance another paradox: the most effective deterrent to conflict is the revelation of comparative strength, which is often only possible through conflict. Yet, as we shall see, this paradox contains elements of great significance for the theory of conflict.

The paradox derives from the fact that conflicts, as distinct from other forms of interaction, always involve power and that it is difficult to appraise the relative power of the contenders before a conflict has settled the issue.

Whatever the goals of conflicting parties, power (the chance to influence the behavior of others in accord with one's own wishes)[35] is necessary for their accomplishment.

We must distinguish here between conflict and contest.[36] In a contest, the winner can be determined according to previously specified criteria against which the contenders are being measured. The one who most successfully meets these criteria—the fastest runner, the most effective writer, the best jumper—is then declared the winner. But in conflict such criteria are not readily available to the contenders. This does not mean, of course, that they are nonexistent.

To be sure, societies contain mechanisms for the adjudication and adjustment of rival claims and the allocation of resources according to some scale of "merit." Ethical and legal precepts limit the unequal distribution of rights among groups and individuals. One of the major functions of government is the final arbitration of antagonistic interests.

However, since there is rarely perfect congruence between what individuals and groups must do and what they desire to do, as long as there exist felt discrepancies between the amount of power, status and wealth that groups command and the amount that they feel to be due them, assertion of strength is the most effective way of establishing claims. A group that is not able to assert its interests will not gain from others consideration for its claims. As Sumner put it with his customary shrewdness: "No doctrine that a true adjustment of interest follows from the free play of interest can be construed to mean that an interest which is neglected will get its right."[37] To make oneself understood and to get others to listen is not unconnected with the possession of power to give force to one's argument.[38]

In conflict, as distinct from contest, "merit" depends, at least partly, on the assertion of power. Thus if contending groups both claim that they desire a given object, allocation may be determined at least as much by the relative amount of power each contender can marshal, as by any normatively established appraisal of comparative needs.[39] If conflict is to be avoided, some other means for ascertaining relative power must be available. However, it would seem that without actual exercise, only some types of power can be measured with any degree of accuracy. Possibly in the economic order, since money is a common measure of values, estimates of financial power (where it can be isolated from social power) can be made with relative ease. But no common measure, comparable to money, is available for the appraisal of noneconomic power. "No medium of exchange could be devised which would bear the same relation to estimates of fighting power as monetary metals [bear] to estimates of economic values."[40] Power thus is more difficult to estimate than wealth. Simmel implies that this very difficulty is one of the obstacles to the prevention of conflict.

It is necessary to distinguish between conflict and antagonistic interests arising out of the respective positions of persons or groups within the social structure. Given the respective roles of workers and managers in a capitalist society, the interests of labor and management may be said to be antagonistic. Yet conflict between them, as in bargaining negotiations or strikes, may only occasionally characterize their relations. Similarly, on the international plane, national states, having opposed interests, may engage in conflicts only at certain periods. This distinction makes intelligible Simmel's proposition.

If the adversary's strength could be measured prior to engaging in conflict, antagonistic interests might be adjusted without such conflict; but where no means for prior measurement exists, only actual struggle may afford the exact knowledge of comparative strength. Since power can often be appraised only in its actual exercise, accommodation may frequently be reached only after the contenders have measured their respective strength in conflict.

Efforts at mediation or arbitration of antagonistic interests encounter the difficulty that the assessment of the actual power relations between the contenders can hardly be made before their relative power has been established through struggle. "The mediator," says Simmel, can achieve reconcilation only "if each party believes that the objective situation justifies the reconciliation and makes peace advantageous."[41] The difficulty of estimating power explains why the contending parties will frequently resort to "trial by ordeal" in order to make an evaluation possible. "Because exact knowledge as to comparative strength can often be attained only by an actual trial, this may be the only means of satisfying each one that he is obtaining all the advantages he could command through coercion."[42]

If alternative means are not available or are believed to be unavailable, the only way to a reappraisal of the contending parties' power is to use the "weapon of last resort." Thus incompatible goals and interests in industry lead to struggle, which helps to define the comparative strength of the parties.

If conflict is the most effective means of establishing the relative strength of antagonistic interests, it is apparent that such conflict may be an important balancing mechanism within a society. As E. T. Hiller, in his brilliant sociological analysis of the strike, has said: "The strike is a test of economic endurance—a process of attrition—in which the outcome is determined by the relative resources of the contestants."[43] "Each estimates the limits of his resources as compared with those of his opponent and gauges his own inevitable losses against possible gains."[44] "Cessation of hostilities comes at the point of equilibrium in the resources which the parties can enlist. The ensuing settlement is based, not on an application of recognized principles, but on force, whereby each compels the best conditions he can command within the limits imposed by the codes and established assumptions of the inclusive society."[45] "When during times of industrial peace, irritations disturb the established equilibrium to such an extent that overt strife results, settlement must come through a new balancing of all the forces which can be brought to bear upon the issue."[46]

Trial by attrition may thus serve to reveal the relative strength of the parties and, once relative strength has been ascertained, it may be easier for the parties to arrive at new accommodations with each other. The struggle may arise because the contenders reject a previous accommodation, judging that it no longer corresponds to the relations of strength between them. Once the respective power of the contenders has been ascertained in and through conflict, a new equilibrium can be established and the relationship can proceed on this new basis.[47]

To reformulate Simmel's proposition:

Conflict consists in a test of power between antagonistic parties. Accommodation between them is possible only if each is aware of the relative strength of both parties. However, paradoxical as it may seem, such knowledge can most frequently be attained only through conflict, since other mechanisms for testing the respective strength of antagonists seem to be unavailable.

Consequently, struggle may be an important way to avoid conditions of disequilibrium by modifying the basis for power relations.

Conclusions we reached earlier in these pages we now reach again by an alternative route: conflict, rather than being disruptive and dissociating, may indeed be a means of balancing and hence maintaining a society as a going concern.

The foregoing chapter has discussed three different ways in which conflict creates links between the contenders: (1) it creates and modifies common norms necessary for the readjustment of the relationship; (2) it leads each party to the conflict, given a certain equality of strength, to prefer that the other match the structure of his own organization so that fighting techniques are equalized; (3) it makes possible a reassessment of relative power and thus serves as a balancing mechanism which helps to maintain and consolidate societies.

The following chapter will discuss another facet of the integrative functions of social conflict.

CHAPTER VIII

CONFLICT CALLS FOR ALLIES

PROPOSITION 16:

Conflict Creates Associations and Coalitions

"Conflict may not only heighten the concentration of an existing unit, radically eliminating all elements which might blur the
distinctness of its boundaries against the enemy; it may also bring
persons and groups together which have otherwise nothing to
do with each other. . . . Unification for the purpose of fighting
is a process which is experienced so often that sometimes the
mere collation of elements, even when it occurs for no purpose
of aggression or other conflict, appears in the eyes of others as
a threatening and hostile act.

"The unifying power of the principle of conflict nowhere
emerges more strongly than when it manages to carve a temporal
or contentual area out of competitive or hostile relationships.
Under certain circumstances, the contrast between ordinary antagonism and momentary association for purposes of fight can
be so pointed that it is precisely the depth of the mutual hostility
of the parties which forms the direct cause of their joining up.

"Unification for the exclusive purpose of defense probably
occurs in most coalitions of extant groups, especially when the
groups are numerous and heterogeneous. This defense purpose
is the collectivistic minimum, because even for the single group
and the single individual it constitutes the least avoidable test of
the drive for self-preservation. Evidently, the more numerous
and varied are the elements which associate, the smaller is the
number of interests in which they coincide."[1]

PREVIOUS PROPOSITIONS concerned the unifying functions of conflict within emerging or already existing groups, and the so-

cializing effect of conflict upon previously unrelated antagonists. The present proposition treats the unifying function of conflict from a different angle: conflict leads to the formation of associations and coalitions between previously unrelated parties. If several parties face a common opponent, a unifying bond is created between them.

Simmel here is concerned with what Sumner has called "antagonistic co-operation": "Competition for life," which according to Sumner dominates the strivings of all individuals in all societies, leads to co-operation, since each individual realizes that he can achieve his ends more effectively by combining with others. "Combination is the essence of organization, and organization is the great device for increased power by a number of unequal and dissimilar units brought into association for a common purpose." "This combination has well been called antagonistic co-operation. It consists in the combination of two persons or groups to satisfy a great common interest while minor antagonisms of interest which exist between them are suppressed."[2]

As an example of "antagonistic co-operation," consider that when competing entrepreneurs realize that they as entrepreneurs have certain common interests in opposition to the interests of other groups, they may band together in order to defend these interests while continuing to compete with each other in other aspects of their separate existence.

Antagonism against a common enemy may be a binding element in two ways. It may either lead to the formation of new groups with distinct boundary lines, ideologies, loyalties and common values, or, stopping short of this, it may result only in instrumental associations in the face of a common threat. The emergence of such associations of otherwise isolated individuals represents a "minimum" of unification.

Simmel's emphasis on the function of conflict in creating associations points to a unifying aspect of conflict that has often been neglected. Even the creation of merely temporary associations may lead to increasing cohesiveness and structuring of a social system.

Conflicts with some produce associations with others. In modern Western society, conflicts through such associations help to reduce the social isolation and atomization of which so many commentators have for so long made so much. Tocqueville could write about the America of 1830: "Each individual stands apart in solitary weakness,"[3] thus voicing a belief that was to be repeated over and over again in the generations to follow. Yet, as Max Weber saw so clearly, the American structure "did *not* constitute a formless sandheap of individuals, but rather a buzzing complex of strictly exclusive, yet voluntary associations."[4]

Many of these buzzing associations in American society were formed to pursue conflicts arising from special interests.[5] Conflicts of interest arising from purely instrumental considerations of "isolated individuals" have had the unanticipated consequences of creating groups and associations that overcome the very isolation of the individual that disturbed Tocqueville. What Durkheim expected new types of corporative organs to accomplish, has actually been achieved to some degree by the multitude of associations which have sprung from the multiform conflicts of American society. "A nation can be maintained only if there is intercalated a whole series of secondary groups near enough to the individuals to attract them strongly in their sphere of action and drag them, in this way, into the general torrent of social life."[6]

By giving rise to temporary associations, conflict can bind the various elements of society together. It leads to concerted action and gives form and order to what Elton Mayo has called a "dust of individuals." While in social systems governed by ascribed status the individual is embedded securely in well-defined positions, in modern Western society mobile individuals striving for station and status are thrown on their own resources. Instrumental associations in modern society bring structure out of struggle, bring form into what would otherwise be chaos, and socialize individuals by teaching them, through conflict, the rules of social order.

In this work we have sufficiently emphasized that conflict

helps to bring like-minded individuals into more or less permanent groups, which develop their own norms (and possibly ideologies). However, presently we consider areas where such relative permanence of group life cannot be achieved due to certain aspects of the social structure, such as the extreme individualistic character of a culture. In such cases conflict may at least bring about an association of otherwise isolated individuals for the purpose of fighting for a specific goal.

The difference between American and European political parties is best understood by considering the differential impact of conflict on two types of social structure. In Europe, antagonistic interests have generally led to the formation of permanent groupings for conducting political conflict. Because of the relatively strong common bond which their members have felt to exist between them, these groups have generally developed specific ideologies, which strengthen the members' sense of community and thus help to make the struggle more determined. The European political party is generally characterized by its own system of norms and values and by a relatively strong involvement of its members. The American political party more closely approximates an association of otherwise divergent interests than does the typical European *Weltanschauungs* party,[7] although party loyalty to certain—perhaps only vaguely felt—party values is by no means wholly absent.[8] In the United States, with its absence of any trace of feudal elements, perhaps the purest example of a capitalist society, the essentially individualistic orientation toward success is conducive to the associational type of grouping in which the members have no other bond with their fellow-members than the immediate purpose at hand.

A culture with a strong emphasis on pragmatism and instrumentalism, placing a high premium on the success strivings of individuals, is likely to produce a profusion of voluntary associations for instrumental goals. This explains a striking feature of American politics, the extent to which the political party is supplemented by a still looser form of association or coalition: "pressure groups," although these are, of course, not absent in

Europe. Pressure groups consist of otherwise unrelated or even antagonistic individuals and groups, banded together to influence public policy in a direction desired by their members.[9]

Just as conflict may bring together isolated individuals into an association, it may also bring together isolated groups and associations into some form of coalition.[10] The many regional or sectional interest groups in the United States have been moved to coalesce, to band together with other groups of parallel interest, under the impact of felt threats to their existence or the felt need to fight more effectively on the national scene. This has been the history of American sectional farm groups compelled through conflict to combine in national federations. Just as in Europe coalitions were often the only way that a multiple-party system could effectively unite many divergent programs and orientations, so in America coalitions were often the only way in which divergent interests could be effectively united in conflict situations. The Roosevelt coalition of Northern Labor and Southern Agrarian interests in the thirties illustrates this process.

The pressure group, formed to fight specific antagonists or to defend special interests against other interests, is typical of a society in which a general individualistic emphasis makes difficult the formation of more enduring groups which are so much more "demanding" of involvement and participation on their members.[11]

Coalition, as distinct from more enduring types of group formation and unification, permits the coming together of elements that, because of mutual antagonisms, would resist other forms of unification. Although it is the most unstable form of socialization, it has the distinct advantage of providing some unification where unification might otherwise not be possible.

Simmel makes the point that defensive alignments in particular contain only the minimum of unifying elements necessary to conduct a struggle, because participants in such coalitions frequently have only one interest in common: a concern for their "survival" as independent units. The aim of self-preservation alone impels them to enter into a *mariage de raison*.

We see those minimal alignments in a number of international coalitions. The war against Nazi Germany brought into being an alliance of nations with the most various, if not antagonistic, interests and values—including democratic capitalist America; a number of nations that are capitalist but not democratic; and Stalinist Russia, which is neither capitalist nor democratic. The common danger faced by all temporarily obliterated other differences. Each participant fought for survival, but, in order to survive, had to appeal for aid to coalition partners similarly endangered. Only naive observers of the international scene could expect this coalition to endure unaltered after the common adversary was removed and alliance for the sake of self-preservation had receded in importance. The war forced unification, but only the simplest form of unification, coalition, was adequate to the situation, in which some of the partners had little in common except the enemy.[12]

In more general terms, the greater the structural or cultural diversity of those who unite in a coalition, the more their interests other than in the immediate purpose are likely to be divergent if not antagonistic. Such a coalition, if it is not to fall apart, must attempt to keep close to the purposes for which it was formed. Simmel observes elsewhere concerning the structure of large groups: "As the size of the group increases, the common features that fuse its members into a social unit become ever fewer." "Obligatory rules of *every* sort must be the simpler and the less voluminous (other things being equal), the larger the sphere of their application."[13]

In large groups encompassing many divergent elements, the common bond must, says Simmel, be based on the smallest common denominator if the group is not to split up. The present proposition makes the same point with regard to a coalition of otherwise unrelated or hostile elements, and here Simmel's insight about large groups applies with additional force.

In the coalition, which contains even fewer binding elements than the large group encompassing divergent interests, the immediate purpose must be even more exclusively the common bond, since other purposes may activate those hostilities that the members have put aside in order to concentrate on the purpose at hand. If the coalition should diverge from this purpose, it would risk breaking up on the rocks of antagonistic interests of its members. To take any general affirmative action would require a positively stated framework of action. Only activity closely tied to the one purpose of defense permits the realization of agreement.

Now we see why coalitions resist transformation into more permanent groups. They are the simplest form of unification issuing from conflict because they contain an irreducible minimum of unifying elements. Permanent bonds would require the participants to relinquish some freedom of action in the pursuit of group interests. The coalition restricts such sacrifices of freedom of action to the immediate defensive or offensive purpose; it is therefore available to parties that are unwilling to depart from their freedom in any other respect.

Participants in coalition are free to pursue their separate aims in all areas except in that of the common purpose for which the coalition has been formed. When attempts are made to transform such coalitions into more enduring and demanding forms of unification, such as the League of Nations, the United Nations or the various European unification plans, they encounter opposition from "sovereign" states loath to divest themselves of liberty of action against all other nations, including their partners in the coalition.

The rise of Fascism in Europe in the early thirties led to the formation of Popular Fronts, defensive coalitions between various parties of the Left. All attempts to transform these mainly defensive alliances into a more permanent form of unification with positive goals failed, since the doctrinal divergencies and the special interests of the constituent groups imposed insuperable obstacles. Similarly, although the threat of Fascism led in many European countries to United Fronts among Socialists and Communists, all efforts to build a United Labor Party failed completely.

So, a common enemy promotes coalitions, but more than a

common enemy is required to transform coalitions into unified systems or groups. Unification against a common foe tends to remain on the level of temporary association or coalition when it is limited to instrumental ends and temporary, limited purposes. At times, however, common values and norms develop in the course of struggling together. In this event the coalition or association may slowly become transformed into a more permanent group.[14] There may be forces at work within coalitions and especially within associations that press toward a transformation into more permanent groupings. Coalition involves compromise and may promote further compromises, leading to adjustment of interests and values between the partners. Such adjustments may pave the way for even more basic forms of unification.

The likelihood of transformation into more enduring forms of sociation is increased in associations where the members of the alliance are individuals rather than groups. In coalitions, each of the coalesced groups is anxious to maintain its boundaries and the exclusive loyalty of its members. In associations of individuals, however, resistance of this kind is not present, although in individualistic cultures, emphasis on autonomy of the individual may have similar effects.

The history of the American Farmers' Alliance shows the transformation of a coalition. The Alliance had its origin in farmers' clubs whose initial objective was to afford protection against the depredations of cattle and horse thieves and the dangers of losing title to the land because of litigation instituted by so-called land sharks. But soon these clubs began to serve other functions, such as agricultural education, provision of social activities and, in some clubs, co-operative buying and selling. With the great wave of farmers' discontent after the Civil War, the Alliance became first a pressure group and later a political organization. Toward the end of its career, an organization which had arisen out of the need of protection against cattle thieves and land sharks became a party demanding, among other things, free coinage of silver, abolition of national banks, loans on land and real estate, direct election of President, Vice-President and

Senators, universal suffrage, the income tax and the eight-hour day.[15]

The word coalition stems from *coalescere*, "growing together." If an association or coalition endures, it tends to develop loyalties and common norms among its constituents. If an analogy may be used, the horticulturist who grafts a sprig onto a tree knows that in time the close contact will lead to their growing together. Just so, the partners in the coalition or association may come gradually to fit together more closely than before.

The hypothesis quoted earlier, that "if the frequency of interaction between two or more persons increases, the degree of their liking for one another will increase,"[16] although it needed modification with regard to other problems, seems to be applicable here: an increase of interaction between persons or constituent groups in an alliance is likely to increase the strength of sentiment between them, so that they can more readily transform themselves into more permanent groups.

Alliances for the purpose of a specific conflict only, may be said to be inherently unstable types of sociation: either they will dissolve after the accomplishment of the purpose for which they were created, or they will grow into more enduring relations through the gradual adjustment of compromise and the emergence of group purposes, group loyalties and group norms.

The foregoing discussion has been limited in the main to a consideration of defensive alliances. We should have in mind, however, that, as international politics show only too clearly, what appears to be a defensive measure to the coalescing groups or associating persons will seem offensive to the other party in the conflict. Furthermore, as Simmel states, even associations or coalitions that are not set up for conflict purposes at all, may seem threatening and unfriendly to outsiders.

The history of the trade union movement affords a convenient illustration. The formation of trade unions and, later, the attempts to create a *Trades Union*, an amalgamation of existing unions, encountered violent opposition in all western countries precisely because the banding together of workmen regardless of the intentions of the founding members was considered an offensive act.[17] In fact, early unions were primarily mutual aid societies rather than conflict groups.

The threatening impact of associations is of sociological significance, since opposition to the forming of associations is itself creative of new associations. The act of unification, even on the elementary level of coalition or instrumental association, calls forth some kind of unification of those other groups and individuals who feel themselves threatened by the coalition. Employers were moved by the threat of growing trade unions to ally themselves with other employers in order to combat the union "menace." The rise of trade unions stimulated the rise of various types of employers' associations. Moreover (and this is reminiscent of problems discussed in the previous chapter), once these associations had established, through conflict, some rough balance of power, they were led to expect and desire greater unification of their respective antagonists. The clash of interests and the changing balance of power arising from the conflict of associations thus led to an increase in internal unification. Thus the trade unions were gradually transformed from temporary and limited associations into unified groups, and employers' associations likewise acquired more enduring character with specific ideologies and greater centralization of decision-making powers.

In this example, association contained the germ of later, more enduring group formation; but even where this is not the case, the association, by establishing a minimum of bonds between its members, draws them, as well as their antagonists, into more active social life, linking them to the public world of social relations and preventing their withdrawal into the privacy of apathetic isolation.

To reformulate Simmel's proposition:

Struggle may bring together otherwise unrelated persons and groups. Coalitions and temporary associations, rather than more permanent and cohesive groups, will result from conflicts where primarily pragmatic interests of the participants are involved. Such alignments are more likely to occur in flexible structures than in rigid ones, because, in rigid societies, suppressed conflicts, if they break out, tend to assume a more intense and hence more "ideological" character. Coalitions and associations give structure to an individualistic society and prevent it from disintegrating through atomization.

The unifying character of conflict is seen more dramatically when coalitions and instrumental associations produce agreement out of relationships of competition or hostility. Unification is at a minimum level when coalitions are formed for the purpose of defense. Alliance, then, for each particular group reflects the most minimal expression of the desire for self-preservation.

The more the unified elements differ in culture and structure, the smaller the number of interests in which they coincide. Just to the extent that unification is not grounded in prior attraction based on common characteristics will the meaning of unification correspondingly confine itself to coalition and the purpose at hand.

Most coalitions between already existing groups, especially between numerous groups or between those that differ widely from each other, are formed for defensive purposes only, at least in the view of those who enter the alliance. Alliance, even when not formed for the purpose of conflict, may seem to other groups a threatening and unfriendly act. This very perception, however, leads to the creation of new associations and coalitions, thus further stimulating social participation.

CHAPTER IX

CONCLUSION

IN THE PRECEDING PAGES we have examined a series of propositions which call attention to various conditions under which social conflict may contribute to the maintenance, adjustment or adaptation of social relationships and social structures.

We will limit ourselves in these concluding remarks to recalling only some of the results of our discussion, rather than summarizing the content of this book, and will attempt to show that our conclusions fall into a consistent pattern.

Conflict within a group, we have seen, may help to establish unity or to re-establish unity and cohesion where it has been threatened by hostile and antagonistic feelings among the members. Yet, we noted that not *every* type of conflict is likely to benefit group structure, nor that conflict can subserve such functions for *all* groups. Whether social conflict is beneficial to internal adaptation or not depends on the type of issues over which it is fought as well as on the type of social structure within which it occurs. However, types of conflict and types of social structure are not independent variables.

Internal social conflicts which concern goals, values or interests that do not contradict the basic assumptions upon which the relationship is founded tend to be positively functional for the social structure. Such conflicts tend to make possible the readjustment of norms and power relations within groups in accordance with the felt needs of its individual members or subgroups.

Internal conflicts in which the contending parties no longer share the basic values upon which the legitimacy of the social system rests threaten to disrupt the structure.

One safeguard against conflict disrupting the consensual basis of the relationship, however, is contained in the social structure itself: it is provided by the institutionalization and tolerance of conflict. Whether internal conflict promises to be a means of equilibration of social relations or readjustment of rival claims, or whether it threatens to "tear apart," depends to a large extent on the social structure within which it occurs.

In every type of social structure there are occasions for conflict, since individuals and subgroups are likely to make from time to time rival claims to scarce resources, prestige or power positions. But social structures differ in the way in which they allow expression to antagonistic claims. Some show more tolerance of conflict than others.

Closely knit groups in which there exists a high frequency of interaction and high personality involvement of the members have a tendency to suppress conflict. While they provide frequent occasions for hostility (since both sentiments of love and hatred are intensified through frequency of interaction), the acting out of such feelings is sensed as a danger to such intimate relationships, and hence there is a tendency to suppress rather than to allow expression of hostile feelings. In close-knit groups, feelings of hostility tend, therefore, to accumulate and hence to intensify. If conflict breaks out in a group that has consistently tried to prevent expression of hostile feelings, it will be particularly intense for two reasons: First, because the conflict does not merely aim at resolving the immediate issue which led to its outbreak; all accumulated grievances which were denied expression previously are apt to emerge at this occasion. Second, because the total personality involvement of the group members makes for mobilization of all sentiments in the conduct of the struggle.

Hence, the closer the group, the more intense the conflict. Where members participate with their total personality and conflicts are suppressed, the conflict, if it breaks out nevertheless, is likely to threaten the very root of the relationship.

In groups comprising individuals who participate only segmentally, conflict is less likely to be disruptive. Such groups are likely to experience a multiplicity of conflicts. This in itself tends to constitute a check against the breakdown of consensus: the energies of group members are mobilized in many directions and hence will not concentrate on *one* conflict cutting through the group. Moreover, where occasions for hostility are not permitted to accumulate and conflict is allowed to occur wherever a resolution of tension seems to be indicated, such a conflict is likely to remain focused primarily on the condition which led to its outbreak and not to revive blocked hostility; in this way, the conflict is limited to "the facts of the case." One may venture to say that multiplicity of conflicts stands in inverse relation to their intensity.

So far we have been dealing with internal social conflict only. At this point we must turn to a consideration of external conflict, for the structure of the group is itself affected by conflicts with other groups in which it engages or which it prepares for. Groups which are engaged in continued struggle tend to lay claim on the total personality involvement of their members so that internal conflict would tend to mobilize all energies and affects of the members. Hence such groups are unlikely to tolerate more than limited departures from the group unity. In such groups there is a tendency to suppress conflict; where it occurs, it leads the group to break up through splits or through forced withdrawal of dissenters.

Groups which are not involved in continued struggle with the outside are less prone to make claims on total personality involvement of the membership and are more likely to exhibit flexibility of structure. The multiple internal conflicts which they tolerate may in turn have an equilibrating and stabilizing impact on the structure.

In flexible social structures, multiple conflicts crisscross each other and thereby prevent basic cleavages along one axis. The multiple group affiliations of individuals makes them participate in various group conflicts so that their total personalities are not involved in any single one of them. Thus segmental participation in a multiplicity of conflicts constitutes a balancing mechaism within the structure.

In loosely structured groups and open societies, conflict, which aims at a resolution of tension between antagonists, is likely to have stabilizing and integrative functions for the relationship. By permitting immediate and direct expression of rival claims, such social systems are able to readjust their structures by eliminating the sources of dissatisfaction. The multiple conflicts which they experience may serve to eliminate the causes for dissociation and to re-establish unity. These systems avail themselves, through the toleration and institutionalization of conflict, of an important stabilizing mechanism.

In addition, conflict within a group frequently helps to revitalize existent norms; or it contributes to the emergence of new norms. In this sense, social conflict is a mechanism for adjustment of norms adequate to new conditions. A flexible society benefits from conflict because such behavior, by helping to create and modify norms, assures its continuance under changed conditions. Such mechanism for readjustment of norms is hardly available to rigid systems: by suppressing conflict, the latter smother a useful warning signal, thereby maximizing the danger of catastrophic breakdown.

Internal conflict can also serve as a means for ascertaining the relative strength of antagonistic interests within the structure, and in this way constitute a mechanism for the maintenance or continual readjustment of the balance of power. Since the outbreak of the conflict indicates a rejection of a previous accommodation between parties, once the respective power of the contenders has been ascertained through conflict, a new equilibrium can be established and the relationship can proceed on this new basis. Consequently, a social structure in which there is room for conflict disposes of an important means for avoiding or redressing conditions of disequilibrium by modifying the terms of power relations.

Conflicts with some produce associations or coalitions with others. Conflicts through such associations or coalitions, by providing a bond between the members, help to reduce social isolation or to unite individuals and groups otherwise unrelated or antagonistic to each other. A social structure in which there can exist a multiplicity of conflicts contains a mechanism for bringing together otherwise isolated, apathetic or mutually hostile parties and for taking them into the field of public social activities. Moreover, such a structure fosters a multiplicity of associations and coalitions whose diverse purposes crisscross each other, we recall, thereby preventing alliances along one major line of cleavage.

Once groups and associations have been formed through conflict with other groups, such conflict may further serve to maintain boundary lines between them and the surrounding social environment. In this way, social conflict helps to structure the larger social environment by assigning position to the various subgroups within the system and by helping to define the power relations between them.

Not all social systems in which individuals participate segmentally allow the free expression of antagonistic claims. Social systems tolerate or institutionalize conflict to different degrees. There is no society in which any and every antagonistic claim is allowed immediate expression. Societies dispose of mechanisms to channel discontent and hostility while keeping intact the relationship within which antagonism arises. Such mechanisms frequently operate through "safety-valve" institutions which provide substitute objects upon which to displace hostile sentiments as well as means of abreaction of aggressive tendencies.

Safety-valve institutions may serve to maintain both the social structure and the individual's security system, but they are incompletely functional for both of them. They prevent modification of relationships to meet changing conditions and hence the satisfaction they afford the individual can be only partially or momentarily adjustive. The hypothesis has been suggested that the need for safety-valve institutions increases with the rigidity of the social structure, i.e., with the degree to which it disallows direct expression of antagonistic claims.

Safety-valve institutions lead to a displacement of goal in the actor: he need no longer aim at reaching a solution of the unsatisfactory situation, but merely at releasing the tension which arose from it. Where safety-valve institutions provide substitute objects for the displacement of hostility, the conflict itself is channeled away from the original unsatisfactory relationship into one in which the actor's goal is no longer the attainment of specific results, but the release of tension.

This affords us a criterion for distinguishing between realistic and nonrealistic conflict.

Social conflicts that arise from frustrations of specific demands within a relationship and from estimates of gains of the participants, and that are directed at the presumed frustrating object, can be called realistic conflicts. Insofar as they are means toward specific results, they can be replaced by alternative modes of interaction with the contending party if such alternatives seem to be more adequate for realizing the end in view.

Nonrealistic conflicts, on the other hand, are not occasioned by the rival ends of the antagonists, but by the need for tension release of one or both of them. In this case the conflict is not oriented toward the attainment of specific results. Insofar as unrealistic conflict is an end in itself, insofar as it affords only tension release, the chosen antagonist can be substituted for by any other "suitable" target.

In realistic conflict, there exist functional alternatives with regard to the means of carrying out the conflict, as well as with regard to accomplishing desired results short of conflict; in nonrealistic conflict, on the other hand, there exist only functional alternatives in the choice of antagonists.

Our hypothesis, that the need for safety-valve institutions increases with the rigidity of the social system, may be extended to suggest that unrealistic conflict may be expected to occur as a consequence of rigidity present in the social structure.

Our discussion of the distinction between types of conflict, and between types of social structures, leads us to conclude that conflict tends to be dysfunctional for a social structure in which there is no or insufficient toleration and institutionalization of conflict. The intensity of a conflict which threatens to "tear apart," which attacks the consensual basis of a social system, is related to the rigidity of the structure. What threatens the equilibrium of such a structure is not conflict as such, but the rigidity itself which permits hostilities to accumulate and to be channeled along one major line of cleavage once they break out in conflict.

REFERENCES

Preface

1. Robert K. Merton, *Social Theory and Social Structure* (Glencoe, Ill.: The Free Press, 1949), p. 87.
2. Lewis A. Coser, "Toward A Sociology of Social Conflict," (Ph.D. Dissertation, Columbia University, 1954; University Microfilms Publication No. 8639).
3. After this work was substantially completed, we had occasion to read a paper by Jessie Bernard, *Current Research in the Sociology of Conflict* (Working Paper for the Liège Congress of the International Sociological Association, August 24-September 1, 1953, Skrivemaskinstua, Oslo, Norway, mimeo.). It was thus impossible to take Mrs. Bernard's paper into account adequately. Many of my views closely parallel those expressed in this paper, although there exist also a number of divergencies. The reader will find Mrs. Bernard's paper an excellent guide to past research in the area, as well as a stimulating discussion of present trends and future potentialities for research on social conflict.

Chapter I

1. Thomas N. Carver, "The Basis of Social Conflict," *American Journal of Sociology*, XIII (1908), pp. 628-37.
2. Howard W. Odum, "Folk and Regional Conflict as a Field of Sociological Study," *Publications of the American Sociological Society*, XV (1931), pp. 1-17.
3. Jessie Bernard, "Where is the Modern Sociology of Conflict?" *American Journal of Sociology*, LVI (1950), pp. 11-16.
4. The closing sentences of this paragraph are adapted from Robert K. Merton's description of the Puritan ethic in its relation to the cultivation of natural science ("Puritanism, Pietism and Science," in *Social Theory and Social Structure, op. cit.*, pp. 329-46). I believe that the relation between reformist ethic and social science is similar to that between the Puritan ethic and natural science.
5. Again we have adapted two sentences by Robert K. Merton (*ibid.*, p. 331), on the relation of Puritan religion and science.
6. Albion W. Small and George E. Vincent, *An Introduction to the Study of Society* (New York: American Book Co., 1894), p. 77.

7. Charles H. Cooley, *Social Process* (New York: Scribner's Sons, 1918), p. 39.

8. *Ibid.*

9. Albion W. Small, *General Sociology* (Chicago: University of Chicago Press, 1905), p. 205.

10. Edward A. Ross, *The Principles of Sociology* (New York: The Century Co., 1920), p. 162.

11. William G. Sumner, *Folkways* (New York and Boston: Ginn & Co., 1906), p. 12.

12. Robert E. Park and Ernest W. Burgess, *Introduction to the Science of Society* (Chicago: University of Chicago Press, 1921).

13. *Ibid.*, p. 578.

14. Robert E. Park, "The Social Function of War," *American Journal of Sociology*, XLVI (1941), pp. 551-70.

15. A similar idea has been expressed by Philip Rieff in his perceptive article, "History, Psychoanalysis and the Social Sciences," *Ethics*, LXIII (1953), pp. 107-20.

16. Charles H. Cooley, *Social Organization* (New York: Scribner's Sons, 1909), p. 199.

17. Lewis A. Coser, "Toward a Sociology of Social Conflict," *op. cit.*

18. Talcott Parsons, *The Structure of Social Action* (Glencoe, Ill.: The Free Press, 1949).

19. Cf. Robert K. Merton, *Social Theory and Social Structure, op. cit.*, esp. pp. 35 ff.

20. Max Weber, *The Methodology of the Social Sciences*, trans. and ed. Edward A. Shils and Henry A. Finch (Glencoe, Ill.: The Free Press, 1949), pp. 26-27.

21. *Troilus and Cressida*, I, 3.

22. Talcott Parsons, "Racial and Religious Differences as Factors in Group Tension," in Bryson, Finkelstein and MacIver (eds.), *Approaches to National Unity* (New York: Harper Bros., 1945), pp. 182-99.

23. Talcott Parsons, *Essays in Sociological Theory Pure and Applied* (Glencoe, Ill.: The Free Press, 1949).

24. Talcott Parsons, *The Social System* (Glencoe, Ill.: The Free Press, 1951).

25. Talcott Parsons, "Social Classes and Class Conflict," *American Economic Review*, XXXIX (1949), pp. 16-26.

26. Talcott Parsons, *Essays in Sociological Theory Pure and Applied*, *op. cit.*, pp. 275-310.

27. George A. Lundberg, *The Foundations of Sociology* (New York: The Macmillan Co., 1939).

28. F. J. Roethlisberger, *Management and Morale* (Cambridge: Harvard University Press, 1946), p. 112.

29. See esp. W. Lloyd Warner and associates, *Democracy in Jonesville* (New York: Harper Bros., 1949), Chapter XVI.

30. W. Lloyd Warner and J. O. Low, *The Social System of the Modern Factory* (New Haven: Yale University Press, 1947).

31. Kurt Lewin, *Resolving Social Conflicts* (New York: Harper Bros., 1948), p. 163.

32. Kurt Lewin, *The Research Center for Group Dynamics, Sociometry Monographs No. 17* (New York: Beacon House, 1947), p. 7.

33. Kurt Lewin, "Action Research and Minority Problems," *Journal of Social Issues*, II (1946), pp. 34-36.

34. Robert K. Merton and Daniel Lerner, "Social Scientists and Research Policy," in Lerner and Lasswell (eds.), *The Policy Sciences* (Palo Alto: Stanford University Press, 1951), p. 293.

35. Georg Simmel, *Conflict*, trans. Kurt H. Wolff (Glencoe, Ill.: The Free Press, 1955).

36. Georg Simmel, "Nachgelassenes Tagebuch," in *Logos, Internationale Zeitschrift fuer Philosophie der Kultur*, VIII (1919), p. 121.

37. José Ortega y Gasset, "In Search of Goethe from Within," *Partisan Review*, XVI (1949), p. 1166.

Chapter II

1. Simmel, *Conflict, op. cit.*, pp. 17-18.

2. See in this respect Talcott Parsons and Edward A. Shils, "Values, Motives and Systems of Action," in *Toward a General Theory of Action* (Cambridge: Harvard University Press, 1952), esp. p. 109.

3. Especially the work of Jean Piaget.

4. *Soziologie* (Leipzig: Duncker and Humblot, 1908), pp. 610-11.

5. Sumner, *Folkways, op. cit.*, pp. 12-13.

6. Talcott Parsons, *The Social System, op. cit.*, p. 482. Cf. also Talcott Parsons and Edward A. Shils in *Toward a General Theory of Action* (*op. cit.*, p. 108), stressing the crucial significance of boundary-maintaining mechanisms for the maintenance of equilibrium of social as well as biological systems, but failing to mention conflict as one such mechanism.

7. The concept of boundary lines, used by Simmel, seems to need clarification. By boundary line is here meant the differentiation of a clearly defined aggregate of individuals from other such aggregates in such a way that these individuals constitute a group with more or less enduring interaction and relative constancy of pattern. The concept does not imply that such differentiation is based on unchanging structures of relationships between groups or that the movement of persons from one group to the other is impossible; relative constancy of group pattern and clearly defined membership are alone implied.

8. Georg Sorel, *Reflections on Violence* (Glencoe, Illinois: The Free Press, 1950).

9. Karl Marx and Friedrich Engels, *The German Ideology* (New York: International Publishers, 1936), pp. 48-49.

10. Sumner, *Folkways, op. cit.*, p. 12.

11. Robert K. Merton and Alice S. Kitt, "Contributions to the Theory of Reference Group Behavior," in *Studies in the Scope and Method of "The American Soldier,"* Merton and Lazarsfeld (eds.), (Glencoe, Illinois: The Free Press, 1950), pp. 101-2.

12. For evidence for the fact that even the Indian caste system actually is not as immobile as often has been claimed, see Kingsley Davis, *Human*

Society (New York: The Macmillan Co., 1949), pp. 378-85. For a more extended discussion, see the same author's *The Population of India and Pakistan* (Princeton: Princeton University Press, 1951).

13. Cf. Max Weber's distinction between caste and ethnic segregation: "A 'status' segregation grown into 'caste' differs in its structure from a mere 'ethnic' segregation: the caste structure transforms the horizontal and unconnected co-existences of ethnically segregated groups into a vertical social system of super- and sub-ordination. . . . Ethnic co-existences condition a mutual repulsion and disdain but allow each ethnic community to consider its own honor as the highest one; the caste structure brings about a social sub-ordination and an acknowledgment of more 'honor' in favor of the privileged caste and status groups." (From Max Weber: *Essays in Sociology*, trans. Gerth and Mills [New York: Oxford University Press, 1946], p. 189.)

14. Lloyd Warner and Paul S. Lunt, *The Social Life of a Modern Community* (New Haven: Yale University Press, 1941), esp. pp. 114-16.

15. Cf. Max Scheler, "Das Ressentiment im Aufbau der Moralen," in *Vom Umsturz der Werte*, Vol. I (Leipzig: Der Neue Geist Verlag, 1923), for the author's detailed discussion of this concept originally derived from Nietzsche. Cf. also Merton's comments in *Social Theory and Social Structure*, *op. cit.*, p. 145, and Svend Ranulf, *Moral Indignation and Middle Class Psychology* (Copenhagen: Munksgaard, 1938), *passim*.

16. The distinction between *attitude* and *behavior* is similar to that between prejudice and discrimination in the sociological study of racial and ethnic relationships. Cf. Robert K. Merton, "Discrimination and the American Creed," in R. M. MacIver (ed.), *Discrimination and National Welfare* (New York: Harper Bros., 1948), pp. 99-126.

17. The existence of such hostile sentiments within the Indian caste structure is perhaps best exemplified by the recent Indian communal riots in which, as many observers have pointed out, violence and brutality assumed—in peace-loving India!—proportions rarely encountered in Western society. Cf. Gardner Murphy, *In the Minds of Men* (New York: Basic Books, 1953), pp. 239-41.

When the suppressed hostility finds a *legitimate outlet*—in this case against the Muslim out-group—it is apt to manifest itself with pecular force.

18. Max Weber, who owed much to both Simmel and Marx (though pursuing a distinctive line of thought), defined classes as emerging from common economic interests, more specifically from conditions on the commodity market. A number of people who have in common a specific causal component of their life chances constitute a class. But Weber differentiates between the objective situation and hostile attitudes, and the acting out of hostilities in conflict. He states that "communal action," i.e., action which stems from the actors' feelings that they belong together, becomes possible only when they distinctly recognize the specificity of the class situation, i.e., the antagonism inherent in the differential life chances. (Cf. From Max Weber, *op. cit.*, pp. 180 ff.)

Chapter III

1. Simmel, *Conflict, op. cit.,* p. 19.

2. Heinrich Schurtz, *Altersklassen und Maennerbuende* (Berlin: G. Reimer, 1903).

3. Alfred Vierkandt, *Gesellschaftslehre* (Stuttgart: Ferdinand Enke, 1928), pp. 304-5.

4. A. R. Radcliffe-Brown, "Social Sanction," *Encyclopaedia of The Social Sciences,* XIII, p. 533.

5. Clyde Kluckhohn, *Navaho Witchcraft. Papers of the Peabody Museum, Vol. XXII,* No. 2 (Cambridge, 1944), pp. 49, 67, 67.

6. Sigmund Freud, "Wit and its Relations to the Unconscious" in *Basic Writings of Sigmund Freud* (New York: The Modern Library), pp. 697 ff.

7. Delbert Miller and William H. Form suggest that swearing on the part of factory workers and soldiers may serve a similar function. See *Industrial Sociology* (New York: Harper Bros., 1951), pp. 291-92. Cf. also Hans Gerth and C. W. Mills, *Character and Social Structure* (New York: Harcourt, Brace and Co., 1953), p. 285, for similar observations.

8. Margaret Mead and Gregory Bateson, *Balinese Character. Special publication of the New York Academy of Science, Vol. II* (1942).

9. See esp. *Civilization and Its Discontents* (London: The Hogarth Press, 1930), p. 86.

10. Cf., e.g., George Orwell's perceptive remarks on the modern detective story in "Raffles and Miss Blandish," in *A Collection of Essays* by George Orwell (New York: Doubleday Anchor Books, 1954).

11. In P. F. Lazarsfeld and F. N. Stanton (eds.), *Radio Research 1942-43* (New York: Duell, Sloan and Pearce), 1944.

12. See in this respect the pertinent comments of Abram Kardiner in his *The Mark of Oppression* (New York: Columbia University Press, 1951).

13. For a brilliant discussion and summary of prejudice studies, see Robin M. Williams, Jr., *The Reduction of Intergroup Tensions* (SSRC Bulletin No. 57), (New York: 1947); see also the *Studies in Prejudice* series (5 vols.), Max Horkheimer and Samuel M. Flowerman (eds.), (New York: Harper Bros., 1950-51).

14. Research directed at such structural factors might possibly validate the hypothesis that the high incidence of prejudice in such social systems as Nazi Germany, and especially its institutionalization, is related to the rigidity of the social structure. In Lewin's experiments with autocratic and democratic groups (cf. K. Lewin and R. Lippitt, "And Experimental Study of the Effect of Democratic and Authoritarian Group Atmospheres," *University of Iowa Studies in Child Welfare,* XVI, No. 3 [1940], pp. 45-198), the children in the autocratic group ganged together not against their leader, but against one of the children. Kurt Lewin, commenting on this study, remarks: "Through combining in an attack against one individual the members who otherwise could not gain higher status were able to do so by violent suppression of one of their fellows." (*Resolving Social Conflicts* [New York, Harper Bros., 1948], p. 80.)

Note also in this context the suggestive if highly speculative remark of the British psychoanalyst John Rickman that some modern political regimes contain institutions serving to deal with discontent by having central authorities divided into two portions, one fixed and one removable (e.g., King-Parliament or Supreme Court-Constitution). The removable portion receives the brunt of people's discontent with the management of affairs. "So long as the removable portion is worth attacking the fixed portion is safe, and there is continuity in political life." Regimes that do not contain such flexible arrangements in their political structure are more likely to foster direction of aggression outward. "Psychodynamic Notes," in Hadley Cantril (ed.), *Tensions that Cause Wars* (Urbana, Ill.: University of Illinois Press, 1950), pp. 196-97.

15. Kluckhohn, *op. cit.*, esp. pp. 68 ff.

16. We propose to use the term *safety-valve institutions* to denote institutions which serve to divert feelings of hostility onto substitute objects (or which provide substitute means for such diversion), or which function as channels for cathartic release, and not to use it to denote institutions which provide for the carrying out of direct conflict.

17. See, e.g., Leonard W. Doob and Robert S. Sears, "Factors Determining Substitute Behavior and the Overt Expression of Aggression," *J. Abn. Soc. Psych.*, XXXIV (1939), pp. 293-313.

18. Sigmund Freud, "Psycho-Analysis," *Collected Papers* (London: The Hogarth Press, 1950), V, p. 121.

19. Sigmund Freud, "The Unconscious," *Collected Papers, ibid.*, IV, p. 112.

20. Cf. Marx's famous remark in his *Critique of the Hegelian Philosophy of Law*: "The people cannot be really happy until it has been deprived of illusory happiness. . . . The demand that the people should shake itself free of illusion as to its own condition is the demand that it should abandon a condition which needs illusion." Karl Marx, *Zur Kritik der Hegelschen Rechtsphilosophie*, in *Marx-Engels Gesamtausgabe*, I, 1 (Frankfurt: Marx-Engels Archiv, 1927), pp. 607-8.

21. Otto Fenichel, *The Psychoanalytic Theory of Neurosis* (New York: W. W. Norton & Co., 1945), p. 563.

22. Simmel, *Conflict, op. cit.*, pp. 27-28.

23. Else Frenkel-Brunswick, "Interaction of Psychological and Sociological Factors in Political Behavior," *American Political Science Review*, XLVI (1952), p. 63.

24. John Dewey, *Human Nature and Conduct* (New York: Modern Library), p. 226.

25. The choice of objects is random on the psychological level, yet not random on the cultural and structural level, since suitability as a target for tension release depends on a number of structural and cultural factors. For a discussion of the large body of work which has been done in the field of object choice for prejudiced reactions, see Robin Williams, *The Reduction of Intergroup Tensions, op. cit.*

26. The distinction which is proposed here is roughly similar to that between instrumental and expressive behavior which informs many aes-

thetic theories. Cf., for example, John Dewey's *Art as Experience* (New York: Minton, Balch & Co., 1935). Some modern psychologists have employed it also. Thus in his article, "The Expressive Component of Personality" (*Psych. Rev.*, LVI [1949], pp. 261-72), A. H. Maslow distinguishes between coping, i.e., the instrumental and purposive on the one hand, and the expressive, i.e., noninstrumental components of behavior on the other. Coping behavior "comes into existence to get something done . . . it implies a reference to something beyond it; it is not self-contained." Expressive behavior, however, "simply mirrors, reflects, signifies or expresses some state of the organism. Indeed, it most often is part of that state."

Similarly, Henry A. Murray ("Toward a Classification of Interaction," in Parsons and Shils, *Toward a General Theory of Action, op. cit.*, pp. 445 ff.) distinguishes between effect needs and activity needs. An activity need is "a disposition to engage in a certain type of activity for its own sake. . . . The satisfaction is contemporary with the activity itself . . . and it can be distinguished from the contentment that follows some achieved effect."

27. Merton, *Social Theory and Social Structure, op. cit.*, pp. 125-49.

28. Clyde Kuckhohn's "Group Tensions" (Chapter IV of *Approaches to National Unity*, ed. Bryson, Finkelstein and MacIver [New York: Harper Bros., 1945]), incidentally one of the very few works in which the distinction between realistic and nonrealistic conflicts is clearly made, supplies one of the most lucid general descriptions of the sources of nonrealistic conflict. Cf. Gordon Allport's discussion of realistic and nonrealistic conflict in *The Nature of Prejudice* (Cambridge: Addison-Wesley Co., 1954), esp. pp. 229-33.

See also Talcott Parsons' article, "Some Primary Sources and Patterns of Aggression in the Social Structure of the Western World" (*Essays in Sociological Theory, op. cit.*, pp. 251-74) for an effort to trace more specifically some of the sources of nonrealistic conflict in the institutional structure of Western societies.

29. See, e.g., Otto Klineberg, *Tensions Affecting International Understanding*, Bulletin No. 62 (New York: SSRC, 1950), and Stuart Chase, *Roads to Agreement* (New York: Harper Bros., 1951).

30. As Reinhold Niebuhr has cogently argued: "Educators . . . underestimate the conflict of interest in political and economic relations, and attribute to disinterested ignorance what ought usually to be attributed to interested intelligence." (*Moral Man and Immoral Society* [New York: Chas. Scribner's Sons, 1932], p. 215.)

31. *Encylcopaedia of the Social Sciences*, XV, pp. 336-37. Theodore Abel, in a study of 25 major wars, states that he found "in no case the decision [to use war] precipitated by emotional tension, sentimentality, crowd behavior, or other irrational motivations." ("The Element of Decision in the Pattern of War," *Am. Soc. Rev.*, VI [1941], p. 855.)

Cf. also Stanislaw Andrzejewski, *Military Organization and Society* (London: Routledge, 1954).

32. Jessie Bernard is one of the very few sociologists who have attacked the psychologistic interpretation of conflict. Cf. "The Conceptualization

of Intergroup Relations with Special Reference to Conflict," *Social Forces,* XXIX (1951), pp. 243-51.

33. Reference is here made to Freud's distinction between statements which are plausible and those which are nonsensical. If "a person comes along who seriously asserts that the centre of the earth is made of jam," the result will be "a diversion of our interests; instead of their being directed on to the investigation itself, as to whether the interior of he earth is really made of jam or not, we shall wonder what kind of man it must be who can get such an idea into his head. . . ." (*New Introductory Lectures on Psychoanalysis* [New York: W. W. Norton & Co., 1933], pp. 48-49.)

34. Delbert C. Miller and William H. Form, *Industrial Sociology, op. cit.,* p. 79.

35. Cf. Reinhard Bendix and Lloyd Fisher, "The Perspectives of Elton Mayo," *Review of Economics and Statistics,* XXXI (1949), pp. 312-19.

36. This explains the total neglect of unions in the original Mayo studies; see Harold L. Sheppard, "The Treatment of Unionism in 'Managerial Sociology,'" *Am. Soc. Rev.,* XIV (1949), pp. 310-13. See also Robert Sorensen, "The Concept of Conflict in Industrial Sociology," *Social Forces,* XXIX (1951), pp. 263-67, and Arthur Kornhauser *et al., Industrial Conflict* (New York: McGraw-Hill, 1954), esp. the paper by Clark Kerr and Abraham Siegel.

37. Roethlisberger and Dickson, *Management and the Worker* (Cambridge: Harvard University Press, 1939), p. 601. See also the critical evaluation of the Hawthorne Counselling Program by Jeanne L. and Harold L. Wilensky, "Personnel Counselling: The Hawthorne Case," *Am. J. Soc.,* LVII (1951), pp. 365 ff.

38. Max Weber, *The Theory of Social and Economic Organization,* trans. Talcott Parsons and A. M. Henderson (New York: Oxford University Press, 1947), p. 92.

39. Emphasis mine—L.C.

40. Emphasis in the original.

41. Talcott Parsons, *Religious Perspectives of College Teaching in Sociology and Social Psychology* (New Haven: The Edward W. Hagen Foundation, n.d.), p. 40.

42. The distinction here proposed is similar to one proposed by Merton in a paper on "Discrimination and the American Creed" (*op. cit.*). Cf. also T. W. Adorno *et al., The Authoritarian Personality* (New York: Harper Bros., 1950).

43. Simmel, *Conflict, op. cit.,* pp. 32, 33, 34.

44. Freud, *Civilization and Its Discontents, op. cit.,* p. 86.

45. See research with children done by Anna Freud, Margaret Ribble, *et al.* See esp. René A. Spitz, "Hospitalism" I & II, *The Psychoanalytic Study of the Child,* I and II (New York: International Universities Press, 1945 and 1946), pp. 53-74 and 113-17, respectively; by the same author, "Anaclitic Depression," *ibid.,* II, 1946, pp. 313-42.

46. René A. Spitz, "Autoeroticism," *ibid.,* III-IV, 1949, p. 119.

47. See esp. Kingsley Davis, "Extreme Isolation of a Child," *Am. J. Soc.,*

XLV (1940), pp. 554-64, and "Final Note on a Case of Extreme Isolation," *ibid.*, L (1947), pp. 432-37.

The two cases of extreme isolation presented in these articles show a significant difference which the author fails to interpret. The first one, Anna, when discovered, "was completely apathetic . . . remaining immobile . . . and indifferent to everything. She could not . . . make any move in her own behalf." Isabel's behavior, on the other hand, "was almost that of a wild animal, manifesting much fear and hostility. When presented with a ball for the first time . . . she reached out and stroked (the investigator's) face with it." The distinction to which the author fails to call attention is that Isabel was capable of aggressive action while Anna was not. This can be accounted for by the fact that "[the mother] and Isabel spent most of their time *together* in a dark room" (emphasis added), while Anna had been kept completely isolated "except for the minimum care to keep her barely alive."

48. Cf. S. Freud, "Why War," *Collected Papers*, V (London: The Hogarth Press, 1950), pp. 273-87; also Edward Glover, *War, Sadism and Pacifism* (London: G. Allen and Unwin, 1933).

49. Bronislaw Malinowski, "An Anthropological Analysis of War," *Magic, Science and Religion* (Glencoe, Ill.: The Free Press, 1948), p. 286.

50. In a series of lectures at Columbia University, 1950-51.

51. John P. French, "Organized and Unorganized Groups under Fear and Frustration," in *Authority and Frustration, University of Iowa Studies in Child Welfare* (Iowa City), XX, pp. 231-308.

52. This finding confirms Simmel's assertion that in-group conflict varies with the degree of stability of the group—a proposition which will be discussed more fully at a later point.

53. French, "Organized and Unorganized Groups under Fear and Frustration," *op. cit.*, p. 287.

54. Stouffer, *et al.*, *The American Soldier* (4 vols.; Princeton: Princeton University Press, 1949-1950), Vol. II, *Combat and Its Aftermath*, p. 166.

55. See comments by Edward A. Shils, "Primary Groups in The American Army," in *Studies in the Scope and Method of "The American Soldier,"* *op. cit.*

56. *The Sociology of Georg Simmel*, trans. and ed. Kurt H. Wolff (Glencoe, Ill.: The Free Press, 1950), p. 147.

57. See, for example, Kurt Lewin, *Resolving Social Conflicts*, *op. cit.*, Chapter 13; also Stuart Chase, *Roads to Agreement*, *op. cit.*

58. *Conflict*, *op. cit.*, pp. 22, 23, 25.

59. The term "ambivalence" was coined by E. Bleuler in 1910, long after Simmel's *Soziologie* had appeared, in a lecture abstracted in *Zentralblatt fuer Psychoanalyse*, I, p. 266; quoted by Freud in "The Dynamics of the Transference," *Collected Papers*, *op. cit.*, II, p. 320.

60. S. Freud, *A General Introduction to Psychoanalysis* (Garden City: Garden City Publishing Co., 1938), p. 370.

61. S. Freud, *Group Psychology and the Analysis of the Ego* (London: The Hogarth Press, 1948), pp. 54-55.

62. As is well known, Freud's discussion of ambivalence stems from

his analysis of relations in that central primary group, the family. Cf. J. C. Flügel, *The Psychoanalytic Study of the Family* (London: The Hogarth Press, 1921).

63. See George C. Homans, *The Human Group* (New York: Harcourt, Brace & Co., 1950), esp. pp. 113 ff.

64. A later proposition will discuss the conditions under which such suppression of antagonistic behavior is more likely to occur.

65. This lack of understanding of the ambivalent nature of human relations has characterized much of small-group research. Thus Leon Festinger *et al.*, in *Changing Attitudes through Social Contact* (Ann Arbor: Research Center for Group Dynamics, University of Michigan, 1951), describe an experiment set up to test the hypothesis that hostility among the members of a group could be reduced through increasing social contacts between group members. The experiment showed in actual fact, in full confirmation of Simmel's proposition (of which the authors, however, were not aware) that increase in contact brought about an increase in hostility. Indeed, the authors ruefully admit that if the project had continued much longer, it would have led to schism and conflict (pp. 70-71).

66. "An Anthropological Analysis of War," *op. cit.*

67. *Ibid.*, p. 285.

68. *Ibid.*, p. 287. This passage represents one of the relatively few comments that Malinowski has made about conflict. In fact, some of the recent criticism of Malinowski makes precisely the point that he was never able to come to grips with the problems of change because he completely focused attention on integration, thus by-passing the analysis of conflict in institutional structures. (Cf. Max Gluckman, *An Analysis of the Sociological Theories of Bronislaw Malinowski*, The Rhodes Livingston Papers No. 16 [Cape Town-London-New York: Oxford University Press, 1949].) Malinowski is attacked for "his refusal to see conflict as a mode of integrating groups and to recognize that hostility between groups is a form of social balance," and because "his concept of institutions as well-integrated units breaks down in the field of social change. . . . It prevents him from fitting in the idea of conflict at all, and stultifies his handling of history." (*Ibid.*, pp. 10 and 16, respectively.)

69. A. R. Radcliffe-Brown, "On Joking Relationships" and "A Furthur Note on Joking Relationships," Chapters IV and V of *Structure and Function in Primitive Society* (Glencoe, Ill.: The Free Press, 1952), pp. 94-95.

70. We had occasion to quote Simmel's view about the alternative between expression of hostility and withdrawal. Radcliffe-Brown offers an interesting confirmation of this idea: he considers that the only other way in which primitive societies can handle the problem arising from the co-existence of disjunctive and conjunctive elements in a relation is by "avoidance taboos," such as the mother-in-law taboo—i.e., by withdrawal (*Structure and Function in Primitive Society, op. cit.*).

Chapter IV

1. Simmel, *Conflict, op. cit.*, pp. 43, 44, 47, 48.

2. In Talcott Parsons and Edward A. Shils (eds.), *Toward a General Theory of Action, op. cit.*

3. See Paul Miliukov, "Apostasy," *Encyclopaedia of the Social Sciences,* II, pp. 128-31.

4. Once a group is well established and its continued existence is no longer in question, it can afford to take a milder view of renegadism. To the modern Catholic Church, "desertion of the faith no longer appears as a vital blow against the survival of the group." (*Ibid.,* p. 130.) As long as the group is still struggling for acceptance, it must mobilize all its energies against the dangers threatening from within. This means that the sharpness of the reaction to the "inner enemy" is in proportion to the sharpness of the conflict with the outer enemies.

This problem will be examined more completely at a later point in this chapter dealing more specifically with the effect on the group of conflict with an outside antagonist.

5. Kurt H. Wolff (ed. and trans.), *The Sociology of Georg Simmel, op. cit.,* pp. 383-84.

6. Scheler, *op. cit.,* p. 89.

7. Cf. Bossuet's dictum, "L'hérétique est celui qui a des idées personnelles."

8. Robert Michels, *Political Parties* (Glencoe, Ill.: The Free Press, 1949), p. 375. (Emphasis mine—L.C.)

9. The perception of danger in this case is analogous to the effects of the "suicidal prophecy," "which so alters human behavior from what would have been its course had the prophecy not been made, that it fails to be borne out." (Merton, *Social Theory and Social Structure, op. cit.,* p. 386.) The fear that the group's unity may be threatened brings about more unity.

10. Recent research in small groups affords evidence to substantiate this point. Thus Leon Festinger, summarizing the result of a series of studies undertaken by the Research Center for Group Dynamics, writes: "The consistent deviate . . . was consistently rejected by almost all of the groups. The variables of cohesiveness of the group and the relevance of the issues to the group did affect the degree to which the deviate was rejected. The highly cohesive group rejected the deviate more than those groups where the issue was largely irrelevant to the functioning of the group. These two factors acted together so that in the low cohesive groups where the issue was irrelevant there was virtually no rejection of the deviate." ("Informal Communications in Small Groups," in *Groups, Leadership and Men,* ed. Harold Guetzkow [Pittsburgh: Carnegie Press, Carnegie Institute of Technology, 1951], p. 41.)

11. Simmel, *Conflict, op. cit.,* pp. 13-15.

12. Kurt Lewin, *Resolving Social Conflicts, op. cit.,* p. 167.

13. José Ortega y Gasset, *Concord and Liberty* (New York: W. W. Norton & Co., 1946), p. 15.

14. John Stuart Mill, *On Bentham and Coleridge,* ed. F. R. Leavis (New York: G. W. Stewart, 1951), p. 123.

15. George Simpson, *Conflict and Community* (New York: T. S. Simpson, 1937), p. 4.

16. Emile Durkheim, *Division of Labor in Society* (Glencoe, Ill.: The Free Press, 1947), p. 129.

17. Wilbert E. Moore, *Industrial Relations and the Social Order* (New York: The Macmillan Co., 1951), pp. 338-39.

18. E. T. Hiller, *The Strike* (Chicago: University of Chicago Press, 1928), p. 125.

John Stuart Mill summed it up neatly when he wrote: "It is the interest of both laborers and employers that business should prosper and that the returns of labor and capital should be large. But to say that they have the same interest as to the division is to say that it is the same thing to a person's interest whether a sum of money belongs to him or to somebody else." (Quoted by Reinhold Niebuhr, *Moral Man and Immoral Society, op. cit.,* p. 153.)

19. Edward Alsworth Ross, *The Principles of Sociology* (New York: The Century Co., 1920), pp. 164-65 (emphasis in the original).

This is not an instance of the convergence between two unrelated thinkers, since Ross knew Simmel's work and was clearly influenced by it. It is rather a case of cumulation in which an original insight has been pushed further by a succeeding thinker.

20. *The Federalist, No. 10* by James Madison already contains the germ of this idea. (*The Federalist,* [New York: The Modern Library, 1937].)

Cf. also Voltaire's dictum that one religion in a country means despotism, two mean civil war, but a multitude mean peace and freedom.

21. Among present-day sociologists, Robin Williams seems to have rediscovered Ross's insight. He writes: "A society driven by many minor cleavages is in less danger of open mass conflict than a society with only one or a few cleavages." (*The Reduction of Intergroup Tensions, op. cit.,* p. 59.) In a more recent work, Williams points out that the multiple overlapping of groups and social categories in American society blurs the sharp edges of potential cleavage: "Without these relatively fluid, crisscrossing allegiances it seems highly probable that conflict would be increased, assuming that class differentiation would not diminish. American society is simply riddled with cleavages. The remarkable phenomenon is the extent to which the various differences 'cancel out'—are non-cumulative in their incidence." (Robin Williams, *American Society* [New York: Alfred A. Knopf, 1951], p. 531.)

22. Simmel, *Conflict, op. cit.,* pp. 46-47.

23. For the distinction between the latent and the manifest, see Merton, *Social Theory and Social Structure, op. cit.,* pp. 21-81; also Clyde Kluckhohn, *Navaho Witchcraft, op. cit.;* for a critical discussion of the limitations of a purely behavioral analysis of sociological data, see Howard Becker, "Interpretive Sociology and Constructive Typology," in *Twentieth Century Sociology,* eds. Gurvitch and Moore (New York: The Philosophical Library, 1945).

24. See, e.g., Ernest W. Burgess and Leonard S. Cottrell, Jr., *Predicting Success or Failure in Marriage* (New York: Prentice Hall, 1939), esp. Chapter IV, "Measuring Adjustment in Marriage."

25. One might note in this connection that people may by-pass the

occasion for conflict not so much because they are themselves insecure about the stability of the relationship, but rather because of the cultural definition of conflict which is generally seen—as in marriage prediction studies—as indicating possible disruption. Thus marriage predictions of the type discussed here may actually serve as "self-confirming prophecies."

26. The forthcoming study in the sociology and social psychology of housing, *Patterns of Social Life*, by Robert K. Merton, Patricia S. West and Marie Jahoda, contains a great deal of pertinent material bearing upon this point. Cf. also the contribution of Jahoda and West, "Race Relations in Public Housing," in *Social Policy and Social Research in Housing*, ed. Merton, West, Jahoda and Selvin, *Journal of Social Issues*, VII (1951), pp. 132-39.

Abram Kardiner, in a psychoanalytical study of Negro personalities, arrives precisely at the conclusion that such ambivalence is prevalent among Negroes. Cf. *The Mark of Oppression, op. cit.*

27. Cf. the insightful little verse that Kurt Lewin liked to quote:

> I was angry with my friend:
> I told my wrath, my wrath did end.
> I was angry with my foe;
> I told it not; my wrath did grow.

Cf. also Terence's dictum: "Animatium irae amoris integratio est."

28. Stouffer, *et al., op. cit.*, Vol. I, pp. 526 ff.

29. Arnold Rose, *Union Solidarity* (Minneapolis: The University of Minnesota Press, 1952), pp. 51-54.

Chapter V

1. Simmel, *Conflict, op. cit.*, pp. 87, 88, 92, 93.

2. Ludwig Gumplowicz, *Der Rassenkampf* (Innsbruck: Maguerische Universitäts-Buchhandlung, 1883).

3. Gustav Ratzenhofer, *Die Sociologische Erkenntnis* (Leipzig: F. A. Brockhaus, 1898).

4. Franz Oppenheimer, *The State* (Indianapolis: Bobbs-Merrill Co., 1914).

5. W. G. Sumner and A. G. Keller, *The Science of Society* (New Haven: Yale University Press, 1927), Vol. I, p. 400.

6. Herbert Spencer, *The Principles of Sociology* (New York: D. Appleton & Co., 1897), Vol. II, pp. 568-642.

7. *Ibid.*, p. 601. Note, however, the qualifications to this generalization in Andrzejewski, *op. cit.*, esp. Chapter V.

8. Alexis de Tocqueville, *Democracy in America* (New York: A. S. Barnes & Co., n.d.), Vol. II, p. 285.

9. *From Max Weber: Essays in Sociology, op. cit.*, p. 261.

10. *Ibid.*, p. 254.

11. See esp. "Politics as a Vocation," *ibid.*, pp. 77-128, and "Bureaucracy," *ibid.*, pp. 196-264.

For a recent extension and discussion of Weber's findings, see Andrzejewski, *op. cit.*

12. Winston Churchill, *The World Crisis*, Vol. IV: *The Aftermath* (London: Butterworth, 1928), quoted by R. K. Merton in *Social Theory and Social Structures, op. cit.*, p. 367.

13. Theodore M. Newcomb, *Social Psychology* (New York: The Dryden Press, 1950), esp. pp. 226-27.

14. Charles H. Cooley, *Social Process, op. cit.*, p. 39.

15. Freud, *Group Psychology and Analysis of the Ego, op. cit.*, p. 53.

16. Andrzejewski, *op. cit.*, p. 121.

17. On Christian sects, the key work is that of Ernst Troeltsch, *The Social Teachings of the Christian Churches* (New York: The Macmillan Co., 1931), esp. pp. 331-43. See also H. Richard Niebuhr's article on "Sects" in *Encyclopaedia of the Social Sciences*, XIII, pp. 624-31, and Ellsworth Faris, "The Sect and the Sectarian," *Publications of the American Sociological Society*, XXII (1928), pp. 144-58.

18. Robin Williams' discussion of the relation of outside conflict and inner cohesion, in his *Reduction of Intergroup Tensions, op. cit.*, with which the writer agrees in the main, fails to make this crucial distinction.

19. See E. Durkheim, *Division of Labor in Society*, for the distinction between organic and mechanic solidarity. Simmel suggests similar ideas; see *The Sociology of Georg Simmel, op. cit.*, pp. 87-104.

20. Cf. D. Feodotoff White's instructive study of the history of the Red Army, which vividly illustrates how the requirements of warfare lead to the transformation of partisan groups into a centralized Red Army: *The Growth of the Red Army* (Princeton: Princeton University Press, 1944.)

Cf. also Andrzejewski, *op. cit.*, who advances a series of historical examples but also notes several exceptions.

21. For recent discussions of the control function of the primary group, see esp. Shils, as well as Merton and Kitt in *Studies in the Scope and Method of "The American Soldier," op. cit.* As to the relation between centralization and conflict in large-scale organizations, Robert Michels' *Political Parties* remains the classic statement. See also Philip Selznick, "Foundations of the Theory of Organization," *Am. J. Soc.*, XIII (1948), pp. 25-35.

What has been said here with regard to the relation between centralization and group structure in the face of outside conflict is not to be construed as a complete acceptance of what Michels calls "the iron law of oligarchy." There is agreement with Michels that centralizing tendencies in large-scale organizations, especially if they are engaged in continuous struggle with outside groups, are neither arbitrary nor accidental nor temporary, but inherent in the nature of the organization and in the nature of its conflict relations. Yet recognition of the existence and relevance of centralizing tendencies does not commit one to the view that "the majority of human beings, in a condition of eternal tutelage, are predestined by tragic necessity to submit to the dominion of a small minority, and must be content to constitute the pedestal of an oligarchy" (*op. cit.,* p. 390). A number of recent studies (e.g., Seymour M. Lipset, *Agrarian Socialism* [Berkeley: University of California Press, 1950], and Rose Laub, "An Analysis of the Early German Socialist Movement," unpub. Master's Thesis, Columbia University, 1951) suggest that countervailing tendencies such as the ideology of the group and the interests of the membership are crucial intervening variables.

22. Cf. Merton's contribution to the restudy of Angell's *The Family Encounters the Depression: A Re-Analysis of Documents Bearing on the Family Encountering the Depression* (New York: Social Science Research Council, 1942). Merton used estimates of family solidarity before the depression in order to predict the probable impact of the depression on family stability.

23. Robin M. Williams, Jr., *Reduction of Intergroup Tensions, op. cit.,* p. 58.

24. Simmel, *Conflict, op. cit.,* pp. 93, 96, 97.

25. At first glance Simmel's assertion that groups engaged in conflict cannot be tolerant may appear open to question. Do not most present-day Protestant sects stress the idea of tolerance as basic to their tenets? Do not liberal, socialist, and most conservative parties emphasize the idea of tolerance? The apparent inconsistency is merely a matter of semantics. Tolerance in the popular sense implies that one wishes the maintenance or creation of such a condition in society that every individual, or every group, will be able to pursue its religious and political aims and values without hindrance. Tolerance thus understood simply implies certain arrangements within the institutions of the body politic for religious or political freedom from civil powers. It must be sharply distinguished from the attitudes of religious and ideological groups toward the ideas and ideals they profess (Simmel's meaning of the term). "Intolerance" is the essence of every religious or secular church or sect as an immediate consequence of its faith that it possesses the only effective means for salvation (cf. Guido de Ruggiero, "Religious Freedom," in *Encyclopaedia of the Social Sciences,* XIII, pp. 233-45).

26. For an excellent account of these theoretical differences, see Bertram D. Wolfe, *Three Who Made a Revolution* (New York: The Dial Press, 1948).

27. N. Lenin, *Collected Works* (New York: International Publishing Co., 1929), Vol. IV, Book I, p. 56.

28. N. Lenin, "What is to be Done?" in *Collected Works,* Vol. IV, Book II, pp. 198-99 and 246.

29. Max Weber, *Wirtschaft und Gesellschaft* (Tübingen: J. C. B. Mohr, 1922, pp. 812-13); see also "The Protestant Sects and the Spirit of Capitalism" in *From Max Weber, op. cit.,* pp. 302-22.

30. Lenin's party changed its character to some extent after the October Revolution; we are concerned here only with the original conception.

31. That this was not the only reason for the exclusiveness of the sect need hardly be stressed here.

32. On the mechanisms of co-optation, see Philip Selznick, *TVA and the Grass Roots* (Berkeley and Los Angeles: University of California Press, 1949).

33. This is achieved by first assimilating the dissenter to the negative reference group. Subsequently, such assimilation often works as a "self-confirming prophecy." Cf. the following attack by Lenin: "Do you see now, comrades of the *New Iskra*, where your turn towards Martynovism has landed you? Do you understand that your political philosophy has turned out to be a rehash of the *Osvobozhdeniye* philosophy?—and that (against your will and unconsciously) you have found yourselves at the tail of the monarchist bourgeoisie?" (N. Lenin, *Two Tactics* [New York: International Publishers, 1935], p. 61.)

34. *The Sociology of Georg Simmel, op. cit.*, p. 94. See also E. T. Hiller, *The Strike, op. cit.*, p. 71: "In the main the policies of earlier unions fostered strikes more than present-day craft organizations. Because union structure grew so largely out of conflict, it was fashioned for hostile action."

35. Here again Simmel equates two different aspects of group structure, relative size and type of membership participation. We have already indicated that, although there are grounds to expect a relatively high correlation between them, these two factors must be separately analyzed.

36. Simmel, *Conflict, op. cit.*, pp. 97-98.

37. In suggesting that conscious distortion of the social perception of group members may be "political sagacity," Simmel introduces the role of group leaders in the manipulation of the membership's reactions. In all previous discussions, as well as in those that follow, he limits his analysis almost entirely to the impact of conflict on total group structures without differentiating between leaders and followers (although this distinction is the subject matter of other parts of his sociology; see esp. *The Sociology of Georg Simmel, op. cit.*, pp. 181-306). For the time being, this distinction will be omitted in the discussion, since it would involve a new and exceedingly complex field of analysis. At this point we should, however, acknowledge that leaders may have a vested interest in conflict as a unity-producing mechanism so that they may (1) accentuate already existing conflict (as, e.g., the leaders of the Gironde in the French Revolution or the Southern War Party in the Mexican War of 1846) if internal dissension and dissatisfaction threaten their leadership; (2) actually "search for an enemy whenever the esprit de corps threatens to become slack," (Grace Coyle, *Social Process in Organized Groups*, [New York: Richard R. Smith, 1930], p. 161), as the totalitarian leadership did in Germany, Italy and Russia, and as the Czarist police knew well when they invented the "Protocols of the Wise Men of Zion."

38. Gordon W. Allport, *Personality* (New York: Henry Holt & Co., 1937), Chapter 7. Max Weber was the first sociologist to suggest these developments. Cf., e.g., his distinction between those who live "off" politics and those who live "for" politics; the former are organizationally conservative. In order to maintain the structure, they may be led to advocate radical changes of the organization's functions. Cf. *From Max Weber, op. cit.*, esp. "Politics as a Vocation," pp. 77-128.

39. Merton, *Social Theory and Social Structure*, *op. cit.*, Chapter 5.

40. Chester Bernard, *Function of the Executive* (Cambridge: Harvard University Press, 1950), p. 91.

41. Lipset, *Agrarian Socialism*, *op. cit.*

42. One is reminded here of the finding of psychoanalysis that the loss of a hate object may have as serious consequences for the personality as the loss of a love object.

43. Otto Fenichel, "Elements of a Psychoanalytic Theory of Anti-semitism," in *Antisemitism, A Social Disease*, Ernst Simmel (ed.), (New York: International Universities Press, 1946), p. 29.

44. Adorno *et al.*, *op. cit.*, p. 622.

45. *Ibid.*, p. 619.

46. Parsons, *Religious Perspectives of College Teaching*, *op. cit.*, p. 40. Psychoanalytically oriented observers (cf. Leo Lowenthal and Norbert Guterman, *Prophets of Deceit*, Vol. V of *Studies of Prejudice* [New York: Harper Bros., 1950-1951]) have commented upon the similarity of fear of the Jew and the Negro to the well-known parasitophobia symptoms. Yet, anti-Semitism can lead to group formation and identification while parasitophobia cannot. Hence, "fear of Negroes" or "fear of Jews" is more functional than parasitophobia for those who suffer from degrouping.

47. See Merton, "Discrimination and the American Creed," *op. cit.*, pp. 112-13.

48. Thomas P. Bailey, *Race Orthodoxy in the South*, pp. 346-47, quoted by Myrdal, *An American Dilemma* (New York: Harper Bros., 1944), p. 1356.

49. Frank Tannenbaum, *Darker Phases of the South* (New York: G. P. Putnam's Sons, 1924), pp. 8-9.

50. Myrdal, *op. cit.*, p. 591.

51. That this fear of the Negro is one of the favored manipulative devices of the Southern demagogue hardly needs any elaboration here.

52. See the citations of Kurt Lewin *et al.*, *op. cit.*

53. Cf. the highly stimulating observations of J. P. Sartre in *Commentary*, V (1946) pp. 306-16, 389-97, 522-31.

Chapter VI

1. Simmel, *Conflict*, *op. cit.*, pp. 39, 40.

2. Cf. Talcott Parsons, "The Motivation of Economic Activities," in *Essays in Sociological Theory*, *op. cit.*, pp. 200-217.

3. For a perceptive discussion of changes in the notion of property rights in American society, see Wilbert E. Moore, *Industrial Relations and the Social Order*, *op. cit.*, esp. Chapter XXIV. See also Peter F. Drucker, *The Future of Industrial Man* (New York: The John Day Co., 1942), esp. pp. 97 ff., on the "acute discomfort" of today's managers concerning what they themselves tend to consider the "illegitimate base" for their social power.

4. Parsons, *The Social System*, *op. cit.*, p. 135.

5. Cf. Erich Fromm: "Einer der drei Haupttypen der Identifizierung

ist eine bereichernde, d. h. eine Identifizierung, in der ich die Person des Anderen in mich aufnehme und mein Ich durch diese Bereicherung verstaerke . . ." (*Autoritaet und Familie*, ed. Max Horkheimer [Paris: Librairie Felix Alcan, 1936], "Sozialpsychologischer Teil," p. 83).

6. Lewin, *Resolving Social Conflicts, op. cit.*, p. 199.

7. Machiavelli saw this very clearly. Thus he says in the tenth chapter of *The Prince*: "It is the nature of men to be as much bound by the benefits they confer as by those they receive."

8. This is true to some extent even in some large business enterprises, in which "profit-making becomes the sole obligation of a role *on behalf* of the collectivity; it is not orientation to 'personal gain' in the usual sense." (Talcott Parsons, *The Social System, op. cit.*, p. 246.)

9. Preface to *Capital* (New York: The Modern Library), p. 15.

10. The word "advocates" is used here intentionally, notwithstanding the fact that Marx himself would have maintained that such intensification of the struggle is immanent in the historical development.

11. On the sociology of intellectuals, see Robert Michels, "Intellectuals," *Encyclopaedia of the Social Sciences*, VIII, pp. 118-26, esp. for his excellent bibliography. See esp. Karl Mannheim, *Ideology and Utopia* (New York: Harcourt, Brace & Co., 1940) also for complete bibliography; see also Max Weber's discussion of the role of intellectuals in religious movements, in *From Max Weber, op. cit.*, pp. 279-80.

12. Selig Perlman, *A Theory of the Labor Movement* (New York: The Macmillan Co., 1928), pp. 280-81.

13. Joseph A. Schumpeter, *Capitalism, Socialism and Democracy* (New York: Harper Bros., 1942), esp. pp. 145-55.

Schumpeter, however, fails to consider how it was that the European class structures allowed intellectuals to perform their peculiar role in the conflict, whereas in the American structure the role of intellectuals was minimized. The rigidity of Europe's class structure called forth the intensity of the class struggle and the lack of such rigidity in America favored the pragmatism of the American labor movement. Only if this difference in structure is taken into account can the different position of the intellectual of the two continents be understood.

14. See Robert K. Merton, "Science and Democratic Social Structure," in *Social Theory and Social Structure, op. cit.*, pp. 307-16.

15. George Simpson, *Conflict and Community, op. cit.*, pp. 25-26.

Chapter VII

1. Simmel, *Conflict, op. cit.*, pp. 26, 35.

2. Cf. Malinowski's essay on war, *op. cit.*

See also Joseph Schneider, "Primitive Warfare: A Methodological Note," *American Sociological Review*, XV, pp. 772-77.

3. Cf.: "Aggressive behavior may . . . serve the child as a means of winning his way into a group, of bringing himself to the attention of an-

other child." (Arthur T. Jersild, *Child Psychology* [New York: Prentice Hall, 1947], p. 147.)

4. Cf. K. M. Bridges, *The Social and Emotional Development of the Pre-School Child* (London: Kegan Paul, 1931), who points out that aggressive behavior by a child new to a group is in part a means of exploring his social environment, his initial explorations tending naturally to include expressions of hostility as much as any other form of behavior.

5. Alfred Vierkandt (*Gesellschaftslehre, op. cit.,* pp. 307-08) expresses a related thought: that one can feel vulnerable to an attack only if one's self is in some sense dependent on the adversary. If one is totally impervious to the adversary, one cannot feel vulnerable. One's self can be wounded only if one admits the right of the adversary to "have a say" (*mitsprechen*) over the worth of one's person. Thus most social conflict, with the previously noted exception, is dependent on the mutual acceptance of the parties.

Cf. also T. S. Eliot's remark, that "genuine blasphemy . . . is the product of partial belief, and it is as impossible to the complete atheist as to the perfect Christian." (*Selected Essays* [New York: Harcourt, Brace & Co., 1950], p. 373.)

6. Emile Durkheim, *The Division of Labor in Society* (Glencoe, Ill.: The Free Press, 1947). See esp. Book I, Chapter VII.

7. *Ibid.,* p. 215.

8. Malinowski, in a passage directly following the one quoted earlier ("An Anthropological Analysis of War"), makes a similar point: "The very essence of an institution, however, is that it is built upon the charter of fundamental rules which . . . clearly define the rights, prerogatives and duties of all the partners. . . . This does not mean that people do not quarrel, argue and dispute. . . . It means first and foremost that all such disputes are within the universe of legal or quasi-legal discourse." (Pp. 287.)

9. Cf. Quincy Wright, *A Study of War* (Chicago: University of Chicago Press, 1942), Vol. II.

10. K. N. Llewellyn and A. Adamson Hoebel, *The Cheyenne Way* (Norman: University of Oklahoma Press, 1941), p. 2.

11. *Ibid.,* p. 278.

12. Max Rheinstein (ed.), *Max Weber on Law in Economy and Society* (Cambridge: Harvard University Press, 1954), p. 68.

13. Roscoe Pound, "Common Law," in *Encyclopaedia of the Social Sciences,* Vol. IV, p. 54.

14. Walton H. Hamilton, "Judicial Process," in *Encylopaedia of the Social Sciences,* Vol. VIII, p. 450.

15. Cf. the excellent discussion of this point in O. Kahn-Freund, "Intergroup Conflicts and their Settlement," *British Journal of Sociology,* V (Sept. 1954), pp. 193-227.

16. The foregoing discussion has been limited to legal norms and rules. It stands to reason that this discussion also holds true for folkways and mores (as suggested by Weber in the above quotation). It is superfluous to elaborate here on a proposition that seems to be accepted by most sociologists.

17. This aspect of Durkheim's thought has been elucidated by Parsons in *Structure of Social Action, op. cit.,* p. 375.

18. Emile Durkheim, *Division of Labor in Society, op. cit.,* p. 102.

19. Emile Durkheim, *The Rules of Sociological Method* (Chicago: The University of Chicago Press), 1938, p. 67.

20. A passage in Simmel's *Soziologie (op. cit.,* p. 611) not directly dealing with conflict makes his affinity with Durkheim even clearer: "Attacks and use of force among the members of a community have as a consequence the enactment of laws in order to stop this behavior. But these laws, though resulting only from the egoism of individuals, yet express the solidarity and community of interests of the community and at the same time bring them into awareness."

21. The same view is expounded by George Herbert Mead, in his "The Psychology of Punitive Justice," *American Journal of Sociology,* XXIII (1928), pp. 577-602: "The attitude of hostility toward the lawbreaker has the unique advantage of uniting all members of the community in the emotional solidarity of aggression." "Seemingly without the criminal the cohesiveness of society would disappear and the universal goods of the community would crumble into mutually repellent individual particles. The criminal . . . is responsible for a sense of solidarity, aroused among those whose attitude would be otherwise centered upon interests quite divergent from those of each other." (*Ibid.,* p. 591.)

22. We must take exception to George Simpson's criticism of Simmel's conflict theory. According to Simpson (*Conflict and Community, op. cit.,* p. 26), Simmel, although asserting that integration through conflict is a communal integration, actually gives examples of conflict that does not take place within a community but between groups that have no communal basis. Such noncommunal groups may be more strongly unified in themselves, says Simpson, but their conflict leaves them further apart than they were before the conflict. What is integrated here is the triumphant and the defeated group each in itself. To Simpson, Simmel implies (but does not actually formulate the thesis) that only groups that are *ab initio* part of the same community are integrated by conflict.

It is inexact to say that all of Simmel's examples come from uncommunalized groups; some deal with marriage and kinship groups, which are communities *par excellence.* In the present proposition, furthermore, Simmel definitely holds that conflict as such is a socializing element even between initially uncommunalized groups; and he presents examples to this effect.

But, more fundamentally, the central weakness of Simpson's argument derives from his setting up a rigid dichotomy between communal and noncommunal groupings. Belongingness to specific communities is defined differently in different situational contexts; and boundary lines between communities, far from being rigid, vary according to, among other things, the "cutting points" of conflict, as Simmel has shown in the first proposition. It might be fruitful for certain purposes to distinguish between communal and noncommunal conflicts, provided one keeps in mind that this is at best a question of degree and not of kind and that boundary lines of what the parties recognize as communities are perpetually shifting. (Cf. Simmel, *Soziologie, op. cit.,* Chapter VI, on the shifting of group alignments in different situational contexts.)

23. Simmel, *Conflict, op. cit.,* p. 90.

24. Frederick H. Harbison and Robert Dubin, *Patterns of Union Management Relations* (Chicago: Science Research Associates, 1947), p. 184. (Emphasis mine—L.C.)

25. Samuel Gompers, *Labor and the Employer* (New York: E. P. Dutton & Co., 1920), p. 43.

26. Cf. Clark Kerr, "Collective Bargaining in Postwar Germany," *Industrial and Labor Relations Review,* V (1952), pp. 323-42.

27. C. Wright Mills, *The New Men of Power* (New York: Harcourt, Brace & Co., 1948), pp. 224-25.

28. For an interesting case study exemplifying this point, see Clark Kerr and George Halverson, *Lockheed Aircraft Corp. and International Association of Machinists,* Case Study No. 6 of Causes of Industrial Peace (Washington: National Planning Association, 1949), in which the authors describe how management and union leadership collaborated during the war to eliminate a minority of left-wing members from employment and union position so as to maintain "amicable relations." See also Clark Kerr and Lloyd Fisher's discussion of the San Francisco "Multi-employer Bargaining" experiment, in Richard A. Lester and Joseph Shister (eds.), *Insight into Labor Issues* (New York: The Macmillan Co., 1942), pp. 26-61.

29. Joel Seidman, *Union Rights and Union Duties* (New York: Harcourt, Brace & Co., 1943), p. 78. (Emphasis mine—L.C.)

30. Labor relations in Europe, especially in England and Germany, perhaps would afford even better illustrations since they have been governed for a much longer period by centralized agreements among the respective labor and employers' organizations.

31. C. Wright Mills, *The New Men of Power, op. cit.*

32. Cf. Georges Sorel's remark: "As long as there are no very rich and strongly centralized trade unions . . . so long will it be impossible to say exactly to what lengths violence will go. Gambetta complained because the French clergy was 'acephalous'; he would have liked a select body to have been formed in its midst, with which the Government could discuss matters. . . . Syndicalism has no head with which it would be possible to carry on diplomatic relations usefully." (*Reflections on Violence, op. cit.,* p. 95.)

33. *TVA and the Grass Roots, op. cit.*

34. This sentence does not appear in the German version or in the Kurt Wolff translation. It is taken from the somewhat different manuscript that was the basis of Albion Small's translation. Cf. *American Journal of Sociology,* IX, p. 501.

35. Cf. *From Max Weber, op. cit.,* esp. pp. 180 ff.

36. Cf. Robert Bierstedt, "An Analysis of Social Power," *American Sociological Review,* XV (1950), pp. 730-38.

37. Sumner, *What the Social Classes Owe to Each Other* (New York: Harper Bros., 1883), p. 89.

38. See the pertinent comment by Will Herberg, "When Social Scientists View Labor," *Commentary*, XII (1951), pp. 593-95.

39. See Reinhold Niebuhr, *Moral Man and Immoral Society, op. cit.*, esp. p. xxiii.

40. Harold D. Lasswell, "Compromise," *Encyclopaedia of the Social Sciences*, IV, pp. 147-49. The foregoing discussion owes much also to Wilbert Moore, *Industrial Relations and the Social Order, op. cit.*, esp. Chapter XVI.

41. *The Sociology of Georg Simmel*, p. 147.

42. E. T. Hiller, *Principles of Sociology* (New York: Harper Bros., 1933), p. 329.

43. Hiller, *The Strike, op. cit.*, p. 195.

44. *Ibid.*, p. 198.

45. *Ibid.*, p. 206.

46. *Ibid.*, p. 192.

47. Contemporary political scientists, possibly because of their frequent involvement in political struggle, have been much more attentive to conflict in the political sphere than other social scientists in their analysis of social processes. A number of recent studies, in most cases inspired by Arthur F. Bentley's classic *The Process of Government* (new ed.; Bloomington, Ind.: Principia Press, 1949), have explicitly analyzed the balancing functions of struggle between political groups. Cf. David B. Truman, *The Governmental Process* (New York: A. A. Knopf, 1951) and Bertram M. Gross, *The Legislative Struggle* (New York: McGraw-Hill Co., 1953). Cf. also V. O. Key, *Politics, Parties and Pressure Groups, op. cit.*

Chapter VIII

1. Simmel, *Conflict, op. cit.*, pp. 98-99; 101-02.

2. Sumner, *Folkways, op. cit.*, pp. 16-17.

3. Tocqueville, *Democracy in America, op. cit.*, II, p. 353.

4. *From Max Weber, op. cit.*, p. 310.

5. Not all associations are formed for purposes of conflict, although most of them engage in conflict at some time during their existence. Not all common interests involve conflict with other interests, e.g., some hobby groups.

6. Preface to the 2nd edition of *Division of Labor in Society, op. cit.*, p. 28.

7. As Edward A. Shils, in "Socialism in America" (*University Observer*, I [1947], p. 99), puts it: "The American does not identify himself easily with comprehensive collectivities; he tends to be pragmatically matter-of-fact in his judgment of day-to-day events. His criterion is 'what's in it for me?' or 'for us,' and the 'what' is defined in terms of monetary income, goods and quite specific enjoyments. A certain irreducible sensitivity to doctrine is necessary for the political attitude which underlies that type of political party which is bound together by the common acceptance of principles."

8. Cf. Paul F. Lazarsfeld, Bernard Berelson and Hazel Gaudet, *The People's Choice* (New York: Columbia University Press, 1948) on the role of party tradition in voting behavior.

9. For an excellent discussion of the function of pressure groups in American politics, see V. O. Key, *Politics, Parties and Pressure Groups, op. cit.*

10. As a shrewd observer of the American political scene has written recently: "All American politics are a politics of coalition—an incessant search for issues and appeals which will unite different groups of voters." And further: "The American political party is a powerful magnet, which draws together, in constantly colliding coalition, a bewildering variety of conflicting elements." (Samuel Lubell, *The Future of American Politics* [New York: Harper Bros., 1952], pp. 139 and 202, respectively.) Cf. also the striking characterization of American politics by another contemporary political scientist: "Like dancers in a vast Virginia reel, groups merge, break off, meet again, veer away to new combinations." (James M. Burns, *Congress on Trial* [New York: Harper Bros., 1949], p. 33.)

11. The difference between the European and the American labor movements, which has so often startled foreign observers, may also stem, in part, from the American members' reluctance to join more enduring groups. The American union movement arose primarily as a loose federation of craft unions which, in an attempt to control the labor market in their specific crafts, felt the need for coalitions and alliances with other crafts pursuing similar aims in conflict with their employers. The constituent unions in turn were formed in the beginning primarily by those who felt that they could attain their individual goals more effectively by presenting a common front to their employers. In the course of their development, the unions and their federations have assumed more the character of a "movement," i.e., a loose alliance of individuals and groups has grown into an entity with common loyalties, ideologies and objectives transcending immediate instrumental ends. The movement now demands of its members, at least in certain crucial aspects, the sacrifice of immediate instrumental considerations in the name of the pursuit of group purposes. Yet the American labor movement still differs from the European in the persistence of the element of "coalition" and "association."

12. After this was written, we came upon the following quotation from Winston Churchill: "The destruction of German military power had brought with it a fundamental change in the relations between Communist Russia and the Western democracies. They had lost their common enemy, which was almost their sole bond of union." (*Triumph and Tragedy,* in *The New York Times,* November 13, 1953.)

13. *The Sociology of Georg Simmel, op. cit.,* pp. 397-98.

14. For a similar distinction, see Everett C. Hughes, "Institutions," in *An Outline of the Principles of Sociology,* ed. Robert E. Park (New York: Barnes and Noble, 1946), p. 308.

Simmel recognizes that length of sociation in coalitions increases the likelihood of their changing into closer forms of unification. He states that length of association favors more fundamental forms of unification in defensive coalitions that endure over longer periods of time either because there can never be a definite victor—as where employers' federations face a perennial struggle with labor—or because the threats never actually materialize but always remain latent, thus demanding eternal vigilance.

15. Edward Wiest, "Farmers' Alliance," *Encyclopaedia of the Social Sciences, VI,* pp. 127-29.

16. Homans, *op. cit.,* pp. 112-13.

17. For England, see Sidney and Beatrice Webb, *The History of Trade Unions* (London: Longmans, Green and Co., 1920), esp. Chaps. 1, 2, and 3. For a general discussion of reactions to demands of freedom of association, see Harold J. Laski, "Freedom of Association," *Encyclopaedia of the Social Sciences,* VI, pp. 447-50.

INDEX

HM
134
C 74 ▬▬ | 6187

CAMROSE LUTHERAN COLLEGE
LIBRARY

FREE PRESS PAPERBACKS

A Series of Paperbound Books in the Social and Natural Sciences, Philosophy, and the Humanities

These books, chosen for their intellectual importance and editorial excellence, are printed on good quality book paper, from the large and readable type of the clothbound edition, and are Smyth-sewn for enduring use. Free Press Paperbacks conform in every significant way to the high editorial and production standards maintained in the higher-priced, case-bound books published by The Free Press of Glencoe.

Many of these books are available in their original cloth bindings.
A complete catalogue of all Free Press titles will be sent on request

Date